THE VATICAN AND COMMUNISM
IN WORLD WAR II

ROBERT A. GRAHAM, S.J.

The Vatican and Communism in World War II

What Really Happened?

IGNATIUS PRESS   SAN FRANCISCO

Cover by Roxanne Mei Lum
Cover Photo: CNS

Pope Pius XII giving blessing following address
to crowd of more than 300,000 persons who
had come to St. Peter's Square to offer homage
and devotion to the Vicar of Christ in protest
to anti-clerical and anti-Christian campaign by
sector of press financed and encouraged by
Communists and left-wing socialists. December 22, 1946.

© 1996 Ignatius Press, San Francisco
All rights reserved
ISBN 0-89870-549-5
Library of Congress catalogue number 95-79873
Printed in the United States of America

CONTENTS

PREFACE

The discrediting and eclipse of Communism as a world ideology also put in crisis a certain way of writing history. That is why, a half-century after the end of World War II, the search is on for a fresh look. The European intellectual class is dismayed and disoriented. Their world, so dependent on Marxist-Leninist ideas, collapsed around them. In the United States writers never took the measure, ideologically, of the war. Rather, they allowed others to introduce Marxist-Leninist interpretations. The legacy is a massive load of manipulated history and arbitrary readings, with a more or less hidden agenda. Worse still, given the conditions of war, it was easy to put into circulation various hoaxes that got credence then and even later, undetected because they fitted into the conventional Communist way of seeing reality.

One of the victims of this process was the Catholic Church, specifically the Vatican, the Pope. These historical essays illustrate, with chapter and verse, how the Communist interpretation grievously corrupted the record. Communism and its sister ideology, National Socialism, had this in common: a radical and venomous hostility to religion. This showed up at every phase of World War II. It is time for cleaning up the fallout of the defunct ideologies of World War II. The perpetrators of this tenacious campaign of anti-Catholic propaganda were not merely men of Moscow but also their allies and sympathizers abroad. Diplomats and journalists with prepossessions of their own contributed their share.

The material developed here is derived mostly from studies published by the writer over the years in the Rome-based fortnightly *La Civiltà Cattolica.* That work in turn was based on research in the Vatican archives and in official archives of Europe and the United States. It was thought appropriate to make at least part of the documentation available in English.

INTRODUCTION

PIUS XII IN THE FACE OF TWO IDEOLOGIES

For most of the twentieth century, the world of politics and culture saw the continuing rise and also the spectacular fall of two aggressive ideologies. After the French Revolution, were the Bolshevik Revolution and the National Socialist Revolution also the wave of the future? Many thought so, and both causes won over dedicated militants confident of inevitable triumph. Men were fascinated, hypnotized, energized by the vision of a better world according to radical new rules. The intellectual milieu— writers, artists, philosophers—proved to be particularly susceptible.

The dream turned out to be a tragic illusion. Each of the once-imposing movements came to a sudden and inglorious end. The center of world Communism in Moscow collapsed as if of its own weight, without a hand laid on it. The breakup of the Soviet Union, foreshadowed by premonitory tremors on the fringe, such as in Poland and in East Germany, sealed the bankruptcy of the Marxist *Weltanschauung*. Its stunned adepts and sympathizers around the world could only debate among themselves in bewilderment what the future could hold for them. An immense amount of Marxist literature went down the drain as outmoded propaganda. The national parties had to find a new identity. The complicated network of auxiliary structures ("fronts") painstakingly built up in the West over the years as instruments of influence and infiltration in public opinion disappeared off the screen.

As for National Socialism, its course was brief and meteoric but bloody and dangerous for all that. The greatest war in history, with millions of dead, was necessary before it was snuffed out. But can ideas really be conquered by military solutions? Nazism was a revolt against the universalizing genius of European tradition. It claimed that the Germanic peoples had been robbed of their identity in the formation of Europe. Among the chief culprits was Christianity, specifically the Catholic Church, hence the glorification of the pre-Christian, pagan, Germanic race. That included, in the theory, various European peoples who did not gladly accept such a linkage, for instance, the Dutch, the Swiss, and all the Scandinavians—not to speak of the English. Alfred Rosenberg was the official spokesman for this racial theory through his book *The Myth of the Twentieth Century,* which was condemned and put on the Index of Forbidden Books in 1934 by Pope Pius XI.

The glorification of the German race allegedly cut off from its roots got adequate expression in the mad course of National Socialism for the cause of neopaganism and racial purity. It led to eugenics, sterilization, elimination of the unfit in gas chambers, and inevitably the expropriation and expulsion of Jews. It led to a relentless struggle to eliminate Christian ideas and Christian influences in the "Volk". And finally, it led to war and the pitiless liquidation of the Jewish populations even outside Germany.

Such, in brief, were the two scourges that flayed society in the twentieth century. So soon after the denouement it is difficult to evaluate the permanent damage that this new invasion of barbarians did to European culture. They left their mark in the history of our times. They did not operate in a vacuum. They reflected, exploited, and probed many aspects, weaknesses, of modern society.

Communism, with Karl Marx, highlighted the social or labor question in capitalist society. National Socialism awakened and pushed to its ultimate the nationalism lurking under the surface throughout Europe. The form it took in Germany proved so venomous because it flourished in a large, industrialized, and well-disciplined base, disoriented by economic distress and the humiliating memory of a lost war, with the inherent leaning for recovery. Under these conditions, nationalism slipped easily into racism.

Marxism and Nazism had the same roots: a materialist, this-world view of the meaning of life. In this perspective a religion, any religion claiming to be supernatural, was a stumbling block, irrelevant, unsocial, inimical. War on religion was essential to the Marxist vision. The Bolsheviks paid dearly in world opinion for the godlessness they openly proclaimed, and they never learned to disavow it.

On the other hand, profiting from the lesson of Moscow, the Nazis were more subtle. They closed no churches, arrested no bishops, the better to mask their purposes, while no less bent on destroying Christianity. They mouthed high-sounding but terribly ambiguous phrases such as "positive Christianity" or others to the effect that everyone could be religious "after his own fashion", as Hitler put it. Later, when the Nazis came to power, they claimed they only wanted to "deconfessionalize public life", a sinister formula that opened the way to all-too-familiar whole-sale arbitrary action. In the same way, they inveighed against "political Catholicism" and denounced the "political churches". They sturdily denied religious persecution while sending priests to concentration camps on pretexts, for example, for misusing the pulpit for political ends or for violation of the currency laws. They wanted criminals, not martyrs. The shell of the Church structure stood up, to mislead, but National Socialism worked mercilessly to undermine its inner life. Small wonder that the Nazis came to be described as "brown Bolsheviks".

The Catholic Church, virtually personifying the religious issue, was a conspicuous protagonist in this twin ideological struggle convulsing Europe, politically and culturally, for the better part of this century. She was the victim of propaganda and tendentious interpretations that varied according to the rapid succession of great events that marked the period. The chief theme was that there was "no persecution" under either Communism or Nazism. The Catholic Church was only "making politics" or worse. A work of review is now in order. Now that Communism and Nazism have gone the way of lost causes, the air is clearer, and the sinister political forces once at work emerge in their true light.

World War II history offers perhaps the most convenient starting point for such a review. Passions and emotions were at their peak. Ideology was never more at work. The atmosphere was ripe for propaganda, for tendentious reporting and interpretation. This situation is particularly true for the classic struggle of the Vatican, that is, of the Pope, with Berlin and Moscow.

The following chapters feature certain significant portions of this drama. For the most part they narrate situations and facts that have generally escaped close inspection by students. These chapters aim to illustrate and correct the many false reports and readings proliferating in the war years. Running throughout, particularly, is evidence of the erroneous suppositions and flagrant lies that too often prevailed on the attitude of the Holy See, the Vatican, toward either Communism or Nazism.

Fixations about the Vatican, products of ideology, propaganda, political speculation, or crass ignorance and bigotry, abounded. And they were not limited to Communist or Nazi sources. A typical and widespread fixation was the pretension that the Papacy was "obsessed" by Communism. The word is pejorative and is meant to be so. It implies a papal monomania, an exaggerated, unreasoning, panicky, narrow-minded reaction to the Bolshevik danger—anything, in short, to put the Church in a bad light without tipping the hand. It is cited compulsively to explain Vatican policy at every turn. The Vatican was "soft" on Nazism because of its "panic" over Communism, and so on. Such a frightening simplification justifies further inquiry into the reality. A wide sector of the intellectual world could look with sympathy on the "noble experiment" in social engineering, whether under Communism or Nazism. That Moscow and Berlin were working for the abolition of religion counted for little in their eyes. Even if, as good democrats, they would deplore Soviet or Nazi excesses, they could not work up particular concern for the fate of religion. On the contrary, Catholic opposition to Communism was decried as reactionary, an attack on progress. In contrast, in the era of appeasement before the war, criticism of Nazism, such as in the 1937 encyclical of Pius XI, was decried even in Britain as narrow-minded clerical interference.

The "obsession" syndrome also turns up in diplomatic correspondence. At the (brief) time of the Soviet-British alliance, it was a convenient epithet on the British side to discount Vatican doubts about the viability of such a union. On the German side, a little later, for the opposite reason, the Reich ambassador to the Vatican chose to tell Berlin about the "nightmare" of Pius XII over the approach of the Red Army. At one time, when it pleased them, the Nazi propagandists could accuse the Vatican of seeking an understanding with the Soviets in order to fight Nazism. This was ungrateful on the Vatican's part, it was said, since it was Nazis who had saved the Church from Communism—a merit that Rome never recognized.

At various times it was asked if the Catholic Church regarded Communism or Nazism as the "greater danger". The question is tendentious and was intended to imply that the Vatican had a choice between the two and that it had to be "soft" on Nazism because it was "hard" on Communism. But the question only has sense, if it has any sense at all, for a very brief period in the last months of the war. Could it refer to the early years when Nazism was just rising and Hitler was discounted? Did it refer to the years of the Spanish Civil War, when both Berlin and Moscow intervened? Could it apply to 1939–41, when Nazism and Communism were joined by a pact of "mutual aggression" against Poland? Did it refer to June 1941, when Britain and anti-Communist Poland were allied to the Soviet Union and the Wehrmacht seemed on the road to victory over Bolshevism? Did it refer to the post-Stalingrad months (1943), when the German forces were in retreat? Did it even refer to 1945, when Berlin was encircled by the Red Army? There was never a question of a Vatican "choice" between two irreligious ideologies equally hostile and dangerous to the future of Christianity.

In most cases the interrogator has in mind solely the point in history at which the Nazi Reich was faltering, after Stalingrad. The tacit or not-so-tacit suggestion is that Pope Pius XII looked to the National Socialists to "save" the Church from the Bolshevism menacing Europe. This is a grotesque image of the Vatican's relations with Nazism, reasonable and logical as it might seem to those who are themselves obsessed by their own "anti-Communist syndrome", and not only in Moscow. Here is one of the egregious distortions of history in need of correction, now that the chief source of the manipulations has gone into the dust bin. A fresh review of the record, clearing out myths and ideology, is all the more timely, in the name of history.

Chapter 1

TOWARD WORLD REVOLUTION
AND THE NEW ORDER

As far as the world Communist movement was concerned, war in
1939 was the prelude to the great revolution foreseen in classic
Marxist doctrine. It was necessarily an "imperialist war" in which
the capitalist regimes—that is, Nazi Germany and democratic
France and their respective allies—would fight each other to
exhaustion, leading to the famous "revolutionary situation". At
this point the working class, under the predestined leadership of
the Communist party, would take power with a "dictatorship of
the proletariat" and inaugurate the classless society. It was a
grand utopia that had seized the imagination of generations since
the Communist Manifesto of 1848. It seemed to be confirmed by
the Bolshevik experience of 1917. Fortified by its supposed mission,
by the power of an idea, Moscow declared war on all things
"bourgeois" from the first days. Among the institutions of the
capitalist world was religion itself, conceived as an instrument of
economic forces. The churches, Orthodox and non-Orthodox,
ranked among the "enemies of the people".

In the 1930s, with the onrush of the economic crisis, the
Marxist vision made more sense; was it more than a utopia? The
result was polarization. The Third Communist International
(Comintern) rose to prominence as Moscow's instrument of
subversion. Based in the Soviet capital, it determined the strategy
and tactics of the national parties. It also expounded authoritatively
the theory of Communism—or, better, its contemporary inter-

15

pretation. From the beginning the world Communist movement was conspiratorial and clandestine. Its program, to put it simply, was openly subversive and revolutionary.

Democracy itself was in crisis. Totalitarianism of the right rose to match the totalitarianism of the left. It came to power on an anti-Communist platform. This took worldwide political form in anti-Comintern pacts. The first such pact was signed between Germany and Japan at the end of 1936. Other countries joined: Italy, Hungary, the Spain of Franco, as also, with the war, Bulgaria, Finland, Rumania, China, and some of the new states of the time. In the terminology of Moscow, this was "Fascism".

One of the most successful initiatives of the Comintern in those years was its call for a "united front" of all leftist movements— parties, organizations, or individuals—to unite in a common opposition against what it called "war and Fascism". It was a new departure particularly in that it solicited even the Communists' hated rival, the Social Democrats. But the appeal was also made to Catholic movements and organizations—the "outstretched hand" (*la main tendue*). The new strategy was adopted by the Communist International in its meeting in 1935. The secretary, Georgi Dimitrov, announced it to the world, and the appeal had an immediate and impressive effect. In France it led to the formation of the popular front coalition of leftist parties that ruled France until the eve of the war. Some Catholic circles accepted the invitation, but most Catholic movements, profoundly diffident, stayed aloof from what was so notoriously of Communist inspiration, even if against "war and Fascism".

The united front tactic, as long as it lasted, exemplified the capacity of the world Communist movement to influence—"to infiltrate" would be the more appropriate term—a wide range of non-Communist circles. But the rising specter of real war in Europe eventually put an entirely new face on the situation. A far more challenging task opened up for the world Communist parties and for the Comintern.

On August 23, 1939, after years of apparently irreconcilable opposition and without advance notice, Adolf Hitler and Joseph

Stalin entered into a treaty of nonaggression and mutual assistance. It was a very distasteful surprise. The orthodox and disciplined party leaders, above all in France, were shaken, mortified, and disoriented. They had no information and no directives from Moscow. Those party members of weak Marxist-Leninist faith quit out of disgust and disillusionment at what they saw as a shotgun marriage. Non-Communist fellow travelers were, of course, even more chagrined and discredited. The disarray on the left was pathetic. Years of work for the "united front against war and Fascism" were washed away overnight. But after only a few days of scrambling into past Moscow declarations in quest of a key, the wise men of the French party found the answer to their dilemma. Stalin, they comprehended, in a genial move had set the stage for the classic "revolutionary situation". The imperialist Nazis and the imperialist democracies were now at each other's throats in the beginning of a predictably ruinous war that would see the end of capitalism and the dawn of the proletarian rising. The Soviet fatherland could stand by, as the *tertium gaudens,* expecting confidently the inevitable denouement foreseen in authentic Marxist-Leninist theory. Before World War II began, Stalin had transformed the imminent clash into an "imperialist war", or so the French ideologues saw it. They opposed the war, courageously biting the bullet, cost what it must, in terms of suppression, arrest, desertion, and treason. The interests of the Soviet fatherland had priority over the interests of France.

Predictably in the face of this demoralizing influence at a time of war mobilization, the French government outlawed the party and suppressed the daily newspaper *L'Humanité,* which went into clandestinity. The final determined gesture of defiance came on October 9, 1939. On that date the ex-Communist deputies, now reorganized under a new name, addressed a letter to Edouard Herriot, president of the Chamber, in which they brazenly demanded that France proceed at once to sue for peace with Nazi Germany. After months of attacking the *munichois* (appeasers), the French Communists were now asking for another Munich. After years of anti-Nazism, they called for surrender to Nazism.

Within a few days the party secretary, Maurice Thorez, deserted his army unit and fled across the border to Belgium. From there he proceeded to Moscow.

Nothing could have emphasized the party's opposition to the war more than the demonstrative flight of the leading French Communist. Thorez was of course condemned in absentia, and he was even stripped of his French nationality. The defense offered by the party is sufficiently revelatory of the thinking of the French Communists at this point. In their clandestine press they were defiant:

> The entire French Communist party expresses its solidarity and its affectionate confidence in its secretary general, Maurice Thorez, whom the French imperialists have condemned to six years in prison, for having taken his post as fighter against the imperialist war and indicating to the workers, peasants, and soldiers that their duty is to organize everywhere, wherever they find themselves, for the struggle against the imperialist war, for peace.

This appeared in the second number of the now clandestine (mimeographed) *L'Humanité*. The organ urged its readers to listen to Moscow radio, giving the times and the frequencies.

And what was Moscow Radio, warmly recommended, saying to its foreign listeners? They were denunciations of France's "criminal war". On February 25, 1940, that is, shortly before the German May offensive, Moscow broadcast, in German, a lecture on "antiwar propaganda in France". The speaker concluded, "The French people are not ready to wage war for the interests of the capitalists. They are waging a heroic struggle against the continuation of this criminal butchery. There is no doubt that the courageous struggle waged by the best representatives of the French people against the imperialistic war will be victorious." After the war the Communists saw to it that nobody recalled that on the eve of France's humiliation Moscow was playing a supporting role in the Nazi defeatist propaganda. In 1914 the Marxist parties in France and Germany dropped their theoretical denunciation of imperialist war to rally to the patriotic cause. It turned out differently in 1939.

In June 1940 France's role in the "imperialist" war was at an end. Feeling itself justified, the party, now on good terms with the occupying Nazis, thanks to Stalin, prepared for the next stage. In a message of October 2, 1940, Maurice Thorez, from his safe haven somewhere, and Jacques Duclos (himself just returned from Belgium), told the party confidently, "Rising against the imperialist war, in which France has been thrust by an unworthy government, supported by a unanimous Parliament, with the exception of the Communists, we have done our duty as proletarian revolutionaries, never forgetting, according to the fine formula of Karl Liebknecht, that 'the enemy is within' [*L'ennemi est chez nous*]." The slogan "*Thorez au pouvoir*" appeared on the walls.

Under the Germans the Communists petitioned for the authorization of *L'Humanité,* naturally in the spirit of the Hitler-Stalin pact, a concession that the new masters of Paris were not yet prepared to grant, pact or no pact. At the end of 1944 Thorez returned to France, hailed in the Communist press in a bare-faced bluff as a "combatant for France". The general public did not know he had been out of the country since 1939. In all those years the party kept up the fiction — "*Thorez au pouvoir*".

The first two years of World War II were in the shadow of the momentous Soviet-Nazi alliance. Nothing was said of the thousands of German Communists languishing in concentration camps. Stalin abandoned them to their fate. Two ideologies supposedly in mortal rivalry agreed to live in peace with each other while they concerted to lay hands on the rest of Europe. Poland was callously partitioned again after a short campaign of days or weeks. Within a few more months France was overrun. At the same time the Soviet Union gobbled up the Baltic states. Britain desperately prepared for a landing on its own beaches, the first since William the Conqueror. Who could oppose this inexorable march across the old continent? "Too little and too late" characterized the military situation from the viewpoint of besieged Britain.

The United States was far away politically and militarily and would remain so for more than these two years. As far as the Holy See was concerned, all this was a disaster of the first order. Two determined and aggressive antireligious forces now had the destiny of the Catholic Church in their hands. The Nazis and the Bolsheviks could do what they wanted, in church matters as in others. The Turkish scimitar hung once more over Christian Europe, and there was no Lepanto in sight.

Pope Pius XI had already, in March 1937, spoken his piece in two hard-hitting encyclicals issued within days of each other, the first, against Communism, "On Atheistic Communism" (*Divini Redemptoris*), and the second, against National Socialism, "On the Condition of the Church in Germany" (*Mit brennender Sorge*), written in German because pointed directly at the Third Reich, its doctrines, and its practices. (The encyclical against Nazism was smuggled into the country and read in the churches before its existence was announced, catching the Gestapo by surprise. Hence, while officially dated before the encyclical against Communism, in fact it was not published in *L'Osservatore Romano* until afterward.) The cardinal secretary of state, Eugenio Pacelli, the future Pius XII, crossed his t's and dotted his i's when as a papal legate to the Eucharistic Congress in Lisieux in 1937 he warned against erroneous doctrines, in particular racism and atheistic materialism — and against subversive tactics such as the Communist "outstretched hand". Two years later these two targets of papal criticism and warnings were masters of Europe.

The stunning and cynical reversal of relationships between Berlin and Moscow could appear merely as the product of the mounting war fever in the aftermath of the Munich crisis. Both London and Berlin courted Moscow. Why Stalin chose the ideologically unlikely link with Hitler has been studied and debated at great length — mostly from the non-Marxist way of thinking. But there is another side. The fact is that Stalin's fateful decision put the Communist parties of the rest of the world in the gravest confusion and danger. A pact with "Fascism"? Was he betraying his own adherents abroad? From the authentic Bolshevik point of

view, of course, it was all amply clear. Or at least the party
ideologues were able to rise to the occasion. The French Communists remained civil toward the occupying forces. In their ever-
present propaganda leaflets and placards they avoided criticizing
Germany. After June 21, 1941, they turned on their erstwhile
friends with fire and fury. The Socialist fatherland was in danger;
ideology was decisive.

Chapter 2

THE USSR AS ALLY:
EMBARRASSMENT IN THE WEST

The ideological crisis in France was not duplicated in Britain. The Communists were not so numerous or so aggressive as on the Continent. The government and the press pretended they did not exist, ignoring (censoring) certain feeble attacks from that quarter on the "imperialist war". No doubt the party had sympathizers. One of the most brazen public voices for the Communist view on the "imperialist war", even in the months of British humiliation, was the bulletin *The Week,* published by Claud Cockburn. He foresaw revolution in the streets of London in the classic Bolshevik tradition. Long after the war it was learned how easily Soviet agents could recruit idealistic Oxford or Cambridge students to become "moles" within the government. In the extremist wing of the trade union movement the Communists had a certain influence, as was tacitly demonstrated, for example, when the government thought it wise to send labor leader Sir Walter Citrine to Moscow, not so much to convince the Soviet worker of Britain's friendly intentions as to ensure industrial peace in the war factories at home.

In June 1941, the Foreign Office and some of the press took it into their heads that Hitler was going to make propaganda profit out of his war in the East by an appeal for Catholic support throughout the world and particularly from the Pope. One is astounded that the Foreign Office was not better informed either of Hitler's real intentions or of the sad state of relations between Berlin and the Vatican, relations so bad that, if comprehended in

London, would have dispelled such a thought from their minds. Today it is clear that the British government had no direct information of any such pious intention on the part of the Nazis. Their worry arose out of a superficial reading of Nazi propaganda, to which their own prepossessions contributed not a little. What they were really worried about was that Catholic opinion in Britain might prove a mischievous obstacle to cooperation with the Soviets. A few phrases from the Pope, they thought, might inflame Catholic resistance to support for Stalin, the archpersecutor. They need not have worried about either the Pope or British Catholics.

If Pope Pius XII were really dominated by an anti-Communist obsession, the new turn in the war, which saw the very life of the Soviet system at risk, should have been an overpowering temptation to betray this publicly. It was not to be. At this point it is relevant to bring to the front what is generally and arbitrarily ignored. There is no trace in the abundant official documentation on either side of any communications between Berlin and the Vatican on such an important matter. This ought to appear very, very strange if not incredible, if indeed the "Führer" intended to wage a war "for Christian civilization". Any serious student of National Socialism, then or later, could scoff at the idea. In short, what is so often found in current comment on the "crusade" is a congeries of propaganda, speculation, wishful thinking, misjudgments, inventions, and falsehoods. Only a Pope calls a crusade, and the voice of Pius XII was spectacularly missing in June 1941. This point was not missed in Polish emigré circles in London at this time, when connoisseurs of Polish literature recalled how the poet Mickiewicz, in his epic *Pan Tadeusz,* put into the mouth of a Polish patriot, at the time of Napoleon's march into Russia: "The Emperor is bound for Moscow! That is a long road if he has set out without the blessing of God." During Napoleon's campaign Pius VII was a prisoner in France. The following recital of developments helps to explain how and why even informed war leaders and their advisors got lost in the pressures and uncertainties of the moment.

Britain, through the mouth of Winston Churchill, wasted no

time in throwing its support to the Soviet Union in June 1941. Militarily and also politically, it made sense. But this new alignment brought problems on the higher plane, raising questions as to the goals of the war. The attack on the Soviets was the first encouraging development since the catastrophe in France, twelve long months before. Britain was still fighting alone, and when Hitler turned to the East the pressure was, for the moment, relieved. Should Hitler enjoy yet another successful Blitzkrieg in Russia, its fate would be desperate indeed.

Churchill himself, an inveterate anti-Communist, declared candidly that he would not unsay a single word he had uttered in the past about the Communist system—but that any enemy of Hitler would get Britain's help. Coming from a politician, this was a logical position. But what caused no perceptible hesitation in the mind and will of a very realistic war leader could remain a troubling question for a vast number of others, in England and elsewhere, for instance, in the United States. When President Roosevelt formally proclaimed the Four Freedoms before the U.S. Senate on January 6, 1941, he never thought of the contingency that within a few months fate or power politics would make the totalitarian Soviet Union one of the sworn allies of the democratic world. The contradictions, hardly resolved by the Roosevelt-Churchill Atlantic Charter of August 14, 1941, were to haunt the Anglo-Americans to the end of the war.

The dilemma of credibility struck Catholic circles. What sense did the war now make? An answer had to be sought and found. The Foreign Office hastened to provide guidelines for the archbishop of Westminster, Cardinal Arthur Hinsley, not shrinking in that urgent moment from proposing their own text for him to pronounce. "I speak as a pastor having only religious and moral considerations in mind" was the introduction the diplomats bravely envisaged to put in the prelate's mouth. Hinsley would be made to affirm that Catholics "can and do support the government and the country's war effort without stint under the magnificent leadership of the Prime Minister, [and] it is clear that the position is unaffected by Germany's action in deliberately bringing Soviet

Russia into the ranks of the attacked nations by an unprovoked invasion."

The Archbishop of Westminster was perfectly able and willing to write such a statement on his own, without waiting for a script to be handed him. No record is found that this draft was ever sent, but it remains a top-level indication of the approach that the government wished to be followed in this awkward moment—by Catholics particularly. It betrays the profound concern in official circles that the "holy war" could split and confuse world opinion. The suggested Westminster statement concluded:

> My last word must be then that Germany's record does not entitle her in any way to be recognized as the champion of Christian Europe. *Non tali auxilio.* Catholics should not let themselves be deceived or confused; by their international record the present German government has blackened the character and blasted the reputation abroad of the German people, among whom live so many millions of fellow-Christians. And even if such a Government should turn round, [and] say that it is now going to break with its past, could anyone with freedom to know the facts and form a judgment upon them be willing to trust Hitler's word? The one word from Germany which does carry conviction to us, and it is repeated again and again by German propaganda, is that the attack on Russia has been launched for the purpose of enabling Germany to pursue to the end her conquest of Great Britain and the British Empire. We are thus warned of our danger. I am confident that our people will meet it with the same calm determination as they have shown since first this war was let loose on the free nations of Europe.

This Foreign Office draft speech was dated June 27. On the same day the British minister to the Holy See, d'Arcy Osborne, was given an authoritative exposé of British policy for explanation to the Holy See. London only indirectly warned against being taken in by Nazi propaganda. It was "sure", it said, that the Vatican would have no difficulty in appreciating "the hypocrisy of the renewed German propaganda to the effect that the Nazis

are the defenders of Christian civilization". At least on this point
the Foreign Office was on the right track. It need have no fear,
although it took them some time to find that out. Is it necessary
to add at this point that Hitler in these days never claimed that
the war on Russia was in any way "in defense of Christian
civilization"? Official Nazi propaganda never made that claim,
limiting itself to allusions to "Europe" or "European culture and
civilization".

What was the origin of this egregious misconception in Whitehall? Did no one in the Foreign Office or the Ministry of Information know even after two years of war that the very idea of
"defending Christian civilization" was completely alien to Hitler's
way of thinking, even as a propaganda gesture?

We are here coming to grips with the fixations, the prejudices,
the prepossessions deeply rooted especially in the intellectual
world, in which the Catholic Church, and above all the Papacy,
is identified as a veritable seedbed of anti-Communist reaction,
because of its long hostility to godless atheism. Add to that the
hereditary anti-Catholicism endemic in Britain.

No less an influential voice than the *Times* betrayed this weak
point in the psychological processes of leading circles. At a
critical moment it allowed itself to publish—because it believed
it—a grotesque account of an alleged interview that Hitler had
given to a German Catholic priest, in which the Führer explained
all his good intentions for the Catholic Church in the war that he
was planning against Bolshevism in Russia. The London newspaper,
in its issue of November 4, 1940—that is, during the London Blitz
and many months before the attack on Russia—reported a "well-
authenticated account" that the German Benedictine monk Dom
Odo had seen Hitler, who gave him this rosy picture of the
future of the Catholic Church in Russia:

We shall recreate the splendid tradition of the Crusades; we
shall carry out our mission to bring civilization to the East of
Europe. A great field of activity will be opened up and
there will be a lot to do for the German Catholic clergy
among people who have run wild and who have been robbed

by Jews and Bolsheviks, not only of their land but of their God.

All the Christian nations—went on Hitler, according to the *Times*—"must be called up and be recruited for the fight against Communism and against the whole concept of Jewish Marxism, which is just as much my enemy as it is the Church's. For this great end you must work among the leaders of Christianity in America."

These words are an imposture that should have defied belief. A worse horror is that knowledgeable Britons, who in these months particularly were stressing Hitler's persecution of the Catholic and Protestant churches, were ready to risk the reputation of their leading newspaper on its authenticity.

Dom Odo, a Benedictine monk of Beuron, in civil life with the title of Duke of Württemberg and related to the British royal family, had been engaged in work for anti-Nazi refugees in Switzerland. But according to the London paper, he was being sent by Hitler in order to persuade the Americans that Hitler was well disposed toward religion. In other words, the scope of the *Times* story (passed, of course, by the censors) was to spike the supposed mission in America, pillorying Odo as a Nazi agent. (This was another serious misjudgment in London. Odo in fact was among the first to reveal to the Americans the program of gassing perpetrated by the Nazis on thousands of handicapped persons in Germany.) The story had the incidental merit of having foreseen in 1940 the Nazi attack of many months later. The rest was an incredibly crass invention. But the *Times* story was picked up by other British newspapers, broadcast by London radio (BBC) to the United States, and also published in the U.S. press. No one could have been more surprised than Dom Odo, barely arrived in New York. He issued an indignant denial. He said he had not been in Germany for seven years, that he had had to flee for his life one step ahead of the Gestapo. As the British ambassador Lord Lothian reported on this subject to London, that seemed to rule out the reliability of the London report.

The *Times* man responsible, Iverach McDonald, has disclosed the origin of this story in his memoirs. He revealed that he got the story from Stefan Litauer, who was working for the Polish government in exile and who seemed so convinced of its authenticity that McDonald felt he had to publish it. (Litauer was an early associate of the Claud Cockburn mentioned at the beginning of this chapter as publisher of the philo-Communist periodical *The Week*.) McDonald wrote:

> It was an odd but vivid story. The chief thing against it was that the Reverend Duke was strongly anti-Nazi. But the Poles were not to be shaken in their information, and we printed the report on November 4. One result was that I received a few weeks later my first letter from a German since the war began. The Duke wrote from across the Atlantic to say he had been dumbfounded to see the report. He had never said anything of the kind.

The story of the *Times* on the imaginary interview of Hitler with a German priest on his good intentions remains a classic specimen of the mechanism and the politics of "information" during World War II. That it was even possible can be charitably attributed to the immense confusion in those dark months of the bombardment of London. Even after the denial, the *Times* man could not disabuse himself of his illusions. If it was not Odo, it must have been someone else. That is, the story was authentic and credible but attributed to the wrong man. McDonald could not resign himself to admitting that what his imaginative and enterprising Polish contact had told him was a fabrication from start to finish. Was the Foreign Office itself any less gullible?

Pius XII, as is evident from his addresses and from the relative Vatican documents, had not for one minute supposed that the new war on Russia was anything but a renewed aggression, without the least consideration for Christianity. "One devil is chasing the other", wrote Monsignor Domenico Tardini, the Pope's top aide on foreign affairs.

The movement Sword of the Spirit took on the task of elucidation. This movement had been founded by Cardinal Hinsley in August 1940, in the dark months of the London Blitz, as a medium for sustaining morale among Catholics. Its objective was "to unite all men of good will in a crusade of prayer, study, and action to combat totalitarian systems, which undermine human society and Christian institutions, and to restore an order of justice and peace". It brought together the brightest lights of British Catholicism, mobilized for the war and the war issues at the religious level. Its function was to expound to the hard-pressed population the moral and spiritual issues of the country's commitment. How was this quite specifically religious activity to justify an alliance with the Soviets, who, after all, represented the same kind of totalitarianism against which the Sword of the Spirit had been writing and lecturing in the past long months? Could one systematically gloss over Soviet atheism and persecution of many decades while at the same time highlighting Nazi paganism and persecution? And that suddenly, overnight, because of a new strategic situation?

The June 26 issue of the bulletin of the movement grasped the nettle. The only possible way of squirming out of the predicament was to make distinctions. Christopher Dawson, a learned historian of European civilization, led off by arguing that the difference between Nazism and Communism is that Nazism is unutterably devoted to the cult of power. "It is not the ideology of the Communist International that Hitler is attacking", he wrote, "but Russia as an independent center of world power." The question for Catholics, therefore, he went on, "is not whether Nazism is preferable to Communism, but whether there can be any truce with a regime which admits no limits and no restrictions on its power".

After this somewhat murky disquisition, Barbara Ward, more journalist and economist than historian, writing in the same issue, felt it was impossible to brush away the similarities between the Communist and the Nazi systems. She quoted Churchill's own view that "the Nazi regime is indistinguishable from the worst features of Communism." However, she added, Communism is not Russia—which had been unjustly attacked. "Even if we were fighting only to defend the rights of the Russian people we should be fighting in a just cause. But we are fighting for the rights of all the peoples of Europe, of all the victims of German aggression—to whom Hitler has seen fit to add the Russians." She exhorted Christians to get rid of their defeatism with regard to Communism. Europe, she assured her readers with a shrewd view of what was to come after the inevitable outcome, would not become Communist because of a victorious Russian army so much as because of anarchy, distress, and lack of any real leadership in Europe after the war.

In another article in the same bulletin of the Sword of the Spirit a year later (July 1942), Ward repeated and refined her thoughts. On the occasion of the Anglo-Soviet treaty, which she approved, she explained:

> But if there are good reasons for welcoming the pact, there are obviously other grounds for misgiving. Moscow remains the headquarters of militant Communism, and Christians in this country, and, indeed, throughout Europe, could not conceivably give their support to this alliance if it were to give official sanction to the spread of Communism. This is at the root of the anxiety that some people feel, for obviously Russia as a national state, or Russia as a heroic fighter in this struggle, is as suitable a partner in any alliance, say, as France or the United States. It is Russia's link with the Comintern that gives reasonable ground for anxiety.

She also returned to the theme of "defeatism" among Catholics. She called for a "spiritual re-ordering of our society".

Both Dawson and Ward thus reflected the widespread concern that the Nazis would try to gain the sympathy of Catholics and anti-Communists throughout the world. Barbara Ward noted, for instance, that Hitler had announced his new aggression in the name of a "holy war" for civilization against Bolshevik barbarism. She warned, "At all costs they [Catholics] must not be used as the spearhead of an infiltration of Nazi propaganda." Such an eventuality was precisely the worry of the Foreign Office.

What the Pope had to say about the new scenario was therefore of the utmost importance. In the first days, Vatican Radio, diligently monitored by the listening services, and *L'Osservatore Romano* offered no clues to Vatican thinking. But then it was announced that on June 29, the Feast of Saints Peter and Paul, the Pope would deliver a radio address titled "Divine Providence in Human Affairs". It can be imagined what speculation such a title at such a moment aroused in the press, already excited enough. Axis circles hoped, and British circles feared, that it might prove to be a papal appeal to cooperate with the Axis in the destruction of atheistic Communism.

In fact, the papal discourse turned out to be a grievous disappointment to the Axis. Herbert L. Matthews, writing for the *New York Times* from Rome, gave his dispatch this lead, which tells all: "Pope Pius XII threw a cold shower over all Axis hopes that he would come out in support of an anti-Bolshevik crusade." He went on to say, "In a world-wide broadcast he made a long and important discourse on the ways of Providence without giving a single word of encouragement to the self-styled crusaders." If the discourse was a welcome surprise in London, it only shows how little even knowledgeable persons (especially in leftist circles, for whom the Pope was only an overheated anti-Communist) understood about the mind of either Hitler or the Pope himself.

The Pontiff alluded to various aspects of the war from the human point of view, but it was not his intention to add fuel to an international political polemic thick with propaganda. The Pope had no need of British warnings. To quote Monsignor Tardini again, "I see the crusade but I don't see the crusaders."

The Italian newspapers ignored the discourse except to give it a brief summary as a religious exhortation. This is the best proof that the Pope had said nothing to their satisfaction. However, this did not prevent (Fascist) Radio Roma from salvaging something, in its English-language transmission of June 30. It said the Pope's words were "quite clearly directed against the Bolsheviks". It found evidence for this analysis in the passage "courage in defense of the fundamentals of Christian civilization and confident hope in their triumph". Radio Roma took this to refer to Italy's part in the war. If the Pope went any farther, it would certainly have cited him. But on the next day the same radio took a different line. In a broadcast of July 1, beamed in English to North America, it said:

> Yesterday [*sic*] the Pope spoke to the world.... His address was highly spiritual, but his words obviously referred to current events. In the past His Holiness had issued encyclical letters strongly denouncing Communism. He referred to the responsibilities of those who have let loose the war. Everyone knows that this is Britain. The Pope also regrets the blockade and counter-blockade. Again, the whole world knows that the blockade was the invention of Britain.

If so little advantage could be extracted from the papal address on "Providence" in the Fascist media, what could the Reich organs say? German propaganda policy at home continued to ignore the Vatican and, above all in this case, to spurn Vatican "help". For foreign consumption, however, some kernels were garnered. In Bern, the *Mitteilungen der Deutschen Gesandtschaft* of July 5 could lead off with a topical subject: "The Crusade against Communism". It began, "The crusade that the new Europe has undertaken under the German leadership against Bolshevism has set all Christendom of the world into immense excitement." This precious piece of propaganda deserves a longer citation:

> Following the ardent aspirations of the Catholic part of Christianity, the Pope himself has now spoken in a meditation full of profound reflections, "On Divine Providence in the Events of Human Life", on the events on the Eastern borders of Europe. In that talk the Pope compared the Moscow of Stalin with the Rome of Nero. He recalled that in either case the pitiless might of the tyrants seemed to triumph over the courage and the spiritual strength of the Christian ranks. Today as before, the Pope continued, Christian culture, love of fatherland, heroic courage, selfless sacrifice, faith, and piety stand against an enemy that brought sin and evil into the very life of the individual, in the sanctity of the family, even into the structure of the whole society. The Pope recalled that this evil and this

exercise of power for a time so dominated that the unbelievers thought they could mock God and his silence and the absence of his power and his Providence.

To this shameless exegesis of the Pope's talk—the like of which was never permitted to be read in Germany—the commentary of the Bern legation added, "Significant here is not only the substance of this pronouncement but also the moment at which the Pope spoke. It was held on the second Sunday of the anti-Bolshevik war and only forty-eight hours after the dispatch of the first Italian volunteer battalions destined for the Eastern front. The blessing of the Pope reached them even before the test of battle." In Switzerland, where this was distributed, the German propaganda services were less zealous in making available the real text of which they made so much. The Catholic daily *Le Courrier de Genève,* replying to complaints of readers on the brevity of the text printed, apologized by saying that "only thirteen lines" had been transmitted by the Swiss Telegraphic Agency and these originated with DNB, the German news service.

It is enlightening and convincing to confront this fanciful version of the Pope's address with a contemporary Gestapo analysis. It took a harsh view of the message. This was communicated by Heinrich Himmler to Foreign Minister Joachim von Ribbentrop three weeks later, on July 21. Himmler saw in the papal discourse nothing but attacks on the Reich. "Significant in this respect is that the Pope, a few days after the outbreak of Germany's fight against Bolshevism, had not a single word against Bolshevism. This fact alone proves unambiguously that his statements were not meant against Bolshevism but exclusively directed against National Socialist Germany." If it were not known that this view came from the pen of Heinrich Himmler, it could be taken for British propaganda.

Chapter 3

PIUS XII AND THE "GREAT DEBATE"
IN THE UNITED STATES

Although the British adjusted themselves to their unexpected
ally without losing a step, the religious issue remained a stubborn
challenge in the following months. In the United States, where
the great debate on American participation in the war raged, the
issue became increasingly acute. Isolationists zestfully exploited
the embarrassment of the interventionists. They scoffed at Britain's
insistence that the war was for human rights and indeed for the
very civilization inspired by Christianity in Europe. President
Roosevelt's proposed legislation for military and economic aid to
the Soviet Union through Lend-Lease offered the occasion for
head-on debate. Even nonisolationists thought that it was not
unreasonable to expect the Soviet leader, Josef Stalin, to make
some gestures in the realm of religious freedom in return for such
aid. The United States, after all, was not in the same desperate
predicament as Great Britain and was not in a state of war. Both
Catholic and Protestant spokesmen, in consequence, asked that
religious liberty be restored in Soviet Russia as a condition for help.

A particularly difficult nut for the Roosevelt administration to
crack was a 1937 statement of the late Pope Pius XI on cooperation with Communism. In his encyclical letter "On Atheistic
Communism", of March 14 of that year, the then Pontiff declared,
"Communism is intrinsically evil and no one who would save
Christian civilization may cooperate with it in any manner
whatsoever." This sweeping statement (meant to be a warning
against the "outstretched hand" tactic of the Communist Interna-

tional at that time was repeatedly cited in the autumn of 1941, and not only by Catholic isolationists. Feelings were so strong that in some circles it was argued that U.S. Catholics would have to declare themselves conscientious objectors if their country should become engaged in a war in alliance with the atheistic and persecuting Soviets—"to save Christian civilization".

In the end of August, as plans for aid to Russia were being prepared against increasing opposition, President Roosevelt decided that the time had come for Myron C. Taylor, his "personal representative" to Pope Pius XII, to return to the Vatican. Taylor had not been in Rome for a year, detained, it was said, by ill health. In any event he was now able to take up a new mission. On September 9, 1941, he was closeted with Pope Pius XII. His objective, although he did not quite put in those terms, was to get the late Pius XI off the President's back. "As a measure for coping with serious Catholic opposition to aid to the Soviet Union," wrote Robert Sherwood, the biographer of Harry Hopkins, "Roosevelt decided to send Myron C. Taylor, his special ambassador, on another mission to Rome." In his own description Taylor wrote later more discreetly that it was the religious issues of the war in Russia that brought him to the Eternal City. In the audience, he wrote, the Pope "confirmed the view that the Holy See condemned atheistic Communism and Soviet practices regarding individual liberty, but that, as at all times, the Holy See continued to regard the Russian people with paternal affection".

General matters affecting the war were also raised by Taylor on the President's instructions. One of these was to insist with the Pope that the United States would not stand idly by and allow Hitler to triumph. The Pope's support for the principles of the Atlantic Charter was also solicited. But what FDR needed most of all, and what Taylor succeeded in getting, was a clarification of the troublesome 1937 phrases of the Pope's predecessor. As Sherwood writes:

> He [Taylor] made a supremely tactful and legitimate presentation of the President's case at the Vatican, where he met with a

most sympathetic reception. While the results of this mission were given no great amount of publicity, they were reflected in the attitude of the Catholic hierarchy in the United States and no serious issue was raised over the more than eleven billion dollars of Lend-Lease materials which went to the Soviet Union.

The world press and above all the Axis diplomats were consumed with curiosity as to the purpose of Taylor's return to Rome. Speculation was rife. What got particular attention was a dispatch by the Rome correspondent of the *New York Times,* Herbert L. Matthews, on September 16. He alleged that the President had asked the Pope to declare the war against Nazism a "just war". The Pope's answer was said to have been a polite "no". There was no hint in the *Times* story that the United States was concerned about the attitude of American Catholics, much less about an encyclical of 1937. The correspondent said, however, that Roosevelt had promised he would try to induce Moscow to change its religious policy. As a guarantee of authenticity, Matthews even described how many pages Roosevelt's letter contained as well as how many pages the Pontiff used in his own reply — a picturesque and imaginary detail that could impress the reader but proved nothing. Taylor flatly denied the story.

These were shrewd guesses, nothing more, and they completely failed to divine Taylor's main objective, which was the clarification of the troublesome 1937 encyclical. If American correspondents were so scantily informed, the Axis diplomats and newsmen were equally unable to penetrate Taylor's secret. Bernardo Attolico, Italian ambassador to the Holy See, told Monsignor Tardini on September 5 (even before Taylor's arrival), that he thought it would be enough for Roosevelt to secure "continuance" of the Holy See's silence on the war in Russia. (On Attolico's own efforts, on the contrary, to break the papal silence on the "crusade", more below.) On Berlin's side, the counselor of the Reich embassy to the Holy See, Fritz Menshausen, in a three-page report of September 13, saw enough to point out that domestic politics had much to do with the talks in the Vatican: "Through this gesture Roosevelt wants to display his good relations with the Pope and intends to strengthen his contacts with the Vatican, in the face of the opposition he encounters in Catholic circles against his war policy, and to document and if possible to get some appropriate expression in view of his cooperation with Bolshevik Russia."

This was close enough. But a few days later, the Italian ambassador was reporting to his government:

> I have received from the Pope the explicit confirmation that the Holy See will do nothing more than it has already done, namely, recommend to the Catholics as such, and principally to the bishops, that they keep out of political controversies as much as possible. I am unable to say how much this pleased Mr. Roosevelt's envoy. The impression I received yesterday from one of the Vatican eavesdroppers—the newly created Marchese Travaglini—is that on this point, perhaps the principal one of his visit, Mr. Taylor failed in his purpose.

The impression persisted that indeed Taylor had failed in whatever he was seeking. Thus the correspondent of *Der Bund* of Bern wrote in the issue of October 12:

> After the departure of Myron Taylor it is generally said in Rome (and this is openly admitted in American circles) that the attempt of Roosevelt to convince the Pope of the necessity of American help for the Soviet Union (and the consequent advantage this would be for Catholic mission work there) can be considered to have failed. Likewise the attempt to absolve Russia from blame on religious persecution is seen as a maneuver to influence not only the 22 million Catholics of the United States but also the Catholics of Latin America and Vatican-true Ireland.

Taylor was probably just as happy if people thought he had failed. The Vatican's own documentation has been published, and from this we learn the successive steps that led to a conclusion entirely satisfactory to President Roosevelt. First, the President sought a reaffirmation of the papal bases for peace. This the Pontiff promised to do at the first feasible moment. The second point was summarized as follows: "Interpretation of encyclical of Pope Pius XI as not condemning the Russian people but directed against Soviet practices in respect to individual liberty". The third point in Taylor's exposition concerned an interpretation of the religious (or, better, antireligious) clauses of the Soviet constitution.

It was the cardinal secretary of state, Luigi Maglione, whom Taylor first saw, and at this time he raised the question of the need for a clarification of the encyclical. The cardinal said that he saw no need for any clarification but that the American prelates themselves could clear up the matter on their own. Taylor saw the Pope on the next day, and immediately afterward—that is, on the Pope's instructions—Maglione told Taylor he would instruct the apostolic delegate in Washington, Archbishop Amleto Cicognani, discreetly and confidentially to inform Archbishop Edward Mooney of Detroit, who was chairman of the Administrative Board of the National Catholic Welfare Conference, and also Monsignor Michael Ready, general secretary, and any other bishops who might inquire that "there is nothing in the encyclical against the Russian people" and that while the Pope condemned Communism, he has and can have only "paternal sentiments" toward them. Any public statement, however, should be made as coming from themselves and without involving the Holy See. The appropriate instructions were sent to the delegate in Washington on September 20. Archbishop Cicognani reported he had passed the information to the persons concerned (Mooney and Ready), who recommended as the appropriate person for the purpose the archbishop of Cincinnati, John McNicholas, O.P. He was described as a man of measured judgment who had up to then not been identified with either of the two contending views. His word, it was thought, would command attention.

One can believe that the U.S. Church leaders such as Archbishop Mooney welcomed this way out of a growing dilemma. The unpleasant public controversies among bishops were endangering the unity of the hierarchy and of Catholics in general. Soon, in November, the annual meeting of the bishops was to take place, and a deep cleavage could well develop if some authoritative guidance were not received from the Holy See. The free use made of the disputed quotations from Pius XI, especially by non-Catholic isolationists, was proving divisive and dangerous. At the end of October, accordingly, McNicholas issued a decisive pastoral that effectively concluded the debate. He addressed himself only to the faithful of his own archdiocese, but its effect was to all intents and purposes meant for a wider audience. He said, in particular:

> However strongly we condemn Sovietism and all the satanic crimes that can be charged to it, we must not, from the words of Pope Pius XI cited, ... say that the great and courageous Pope was laying down a course of action governing our country and all other countries regarding every future circumstance whatsoever, especially in a war of defense. Such an interpretation seems to us extreme, and, indeed, unfair to the memory of the glorious pontiff.

On November 16, the assembled bishops issued a statement warning of the twin evils of Nazism and Communism but recalling that Pius XI himself, while condemning atheistic Communism, had expressed his paternal and compassionate benevolence for the peoples of Russia. The implication could not be lost. The legislation on Lend-Lease to Russia passed. In three weeks the United States itself was at war.

Some general aspects of this unusual precedent call for comment. We see that the President of the United States used his contacts, his influence, with the religious leaders of U.S. Catholics on behalf of an admittedly crucial issue of domestic legislation pending before the U.S. Congress. Had isolationists become aware of the true scope of Myron Taylor's voyage to Rome in September 1941, they would certainly have protested it vigorously as an abuse of power. Secondly, we see that Pius XII, despite his official neutrality, made a move distinctly favorable not only to Roosevelt's domestic policy but also to Stalin and Churchill (and by the same token unfavorable to the German-Italian war effort).

The case recalls the intervention of Pope Leo XIII on Bismarck's request in 1878 on behalf of his military budget (the *Septennat*), blocked in the Reichstag by the Center party. The then Pontiff was sharply criticized by German Catholic politicians for allowing himself to be used by the Iron Chancellor for his own personal policies. For U.S. Catholics of Irish origin, Roosevelt's maneuver (had they known of it) would have called up memories of British manipulations in Rome in the nineteenth century and even later against the Irish movement.

The Axis, for their part, had they known of the real nature of the Taylor mission and, worse, of his success, in the shape of Archbishop McNicholas' "spontaneous" pastoral, could and would have bitterly accused Pius XII of committing an unneutral and hostile act in their regard. We can only speculate on the kind of reply the Pope would have given when confronted with his actions. He could, of course, say that the United States was itself a neutral country, with its own diplomatic envoys in Berlin and Rome. He could also have said that he did no more than to tell the American clergy to stay out of politics—a warning that Hitler, who constantly inveighed against "political Catholicism", would have to appreciate. He could also have said that the Pope cannot remain silent when certain political factions misconstrue a papal encyclical in an arbitrary and even damaging sense. If the President derived some political profit from this, no matter. In any event, it remains evident that the Pope did not share the extreme anti-Communism found in parts of the United States. If that had been the case, he could plausibly have answered to Taylor that he should not be asked to interfere in the normal democratic processes of any people. Instead he contributed significantly to Roosevelt's successful drive to extend military and economic aid to the beleaguered Soviets, to Josef Stalin, no less. It was a rare but revealing case in Vatican diplomatic history.

Chapter 4

SPARRING ON RELIGION IN 1941

Taylor's mission was part of a two-pronged move by Roosevelt, who matched this with simultaneous instructions to Lawrence Steinhardt, the U.S. ambassador at Moscow: raise the religious question with the Soviets. And, later, when Averell Harriman went to discuss with Stalin the details of the Lend-Lease aid, similar instructions were given. But could the President expect the same kind of reciprocity from the diffident and suspicious Bolshevik in Moscow that he got from the Pope in Vatican City?

Hints of the President's plan of action first began to appear with his press conference of October 3. Taylor had left Vatican City and had not returned with his personal report. In the meantime it pleased the President to communicate a significant piece of information. The Polish ambassador, J. Ciechanowski, had informed him that as a consequence of the Soviet-Polish treaty of July, some hundred thousand Poles in Russia (prisoners of war, deportees, and internees) who had not been allowed to return home since September 1939 would be formed into fighting units under their own officers and would have their own chaplains. Nothing was said of the fifteen thousand missing officers already liquidated by Stalin's orders at Katyn in 1940. The units foreseen in the treaty were in fact formed. They left the Soviet Union in 1942, passing through Iran. Many of them fought with the Allies in Italy in 1944, notably at Montecassino. The President was also pleased to tell the press that the remaining Polish community in Moscow had been allocated its own place of worship. This was the moment for Mr. Roosevelt to expand on the vexing question of

freedom in Russia in general. He observed that since the Soviet
Constitution declared that freedom of religion is granted, it was
to be hoped that what the Polish ambassador reported might be
"an entering wedge" for the future practice of complete freedom
of religion. He cited favorably the Soviet Constitution, whose
article 124 read, "In order to ensure to citizens freedom of
conscience, the church in the USSR is separated from the state,
and the school from the church. Freedom of religious worship
and freedom of antireligious propaganda is recognized for all
citizens."

The White House correspondents reported these words only
in paraphrase (according to protocol at the time). In their version
Mr. Roosevelt had said the Soviet Constitution was much like the
U.S. Constitution in protecting religion and at the same time
allowing the right to propagandize against it. This simplistic
assertion aroused a storm of criticism and ridicule. Catholic,
Protestant, Jewish, and other spokesmen assailed it as a caricature
of both the law and the facts. "A hollow mockery", exclaimed
the Jesuit Russia specialist Edmund A. Walsh of Georgetown
University. "A ghastly joke, as well as an insult to the American
public", declaimed the famous preacher John Haynes Holmes.
Dean Luther Weigel of Yale University Divinity School, president of the Federal Council of Churches, made a public statement on how different were the two conceptions of liberty. The
New York Times of October 2 editorially deprecated ill-conceived
efforts to base U.S. cooperation with Russia on democratic
principles. It concluded, "If Stalin's Russia is a democracy, then so
is Hitler's Germany." It was in fact easy for specialists in Soviet
Bolshevism to quote Lenin himself in various statements quite in
contradiction to Roosevelt's apologia.

Axis propagandists had a field day. Virginio Gayda, editor of
Il Giornale d'Italia, on October 8 contrasted the President's utterance with the recent mission of Myron Taylor:

President Roosevelt is now at work creating the fiction of an
orientation of the Church of Rome toward the policy of the
Anglo-Saxon powers against the powers of the Axis. His

propaganda is being circulated by underground channels through deceptive rumors that claim that the Pontiff has shown "comprehension" for the Anglo-American-Soviet collaboration and has "appreciated" certain assurances given him by Taylor concerning an intervention by Washington at Moscow that the government accord full religious liberty to its unfortunate citizens.

The presidential spokesman, stung by the criticisms, told reporters later that many of the published reports went farther than what had really been said. The actual transcript was thereupon released, confirming the basic accuracy of the newsmen's paraphrase. For instance, Roosevelt had declared, "Freedom of religion. Freedom equally to use propaganda against religion, which is essentially the rule in this country, only we don't quite put it that way."

Harriman was still negotiating in Moscow. It may be wondered how seriously he pressed Stalin on the religious question. At least one observer on the Moscow scene had his doubts. An articulate witness to the Moscow drama in these days was the American priest Father Leopold Braun, Assumptionist, who was chaplain of the one Catholic church open in the Soviet capital. He recorded his own evaluation of the American effort at this time in a publication of 1959:

> On the morning of September 30, 1941, the late L. A. Steinhardt, U.S. ambassador to Moscow, without previous warning, pressingly invited this writer to come and have a talk with Mr. Harriman. This resulted in a seventeen-minute hasty conversation, in which a general picture of the situation was given of the yearnings of the Russian people for complete religious freedom. Was this not the time to obtain a quid pro quo from the Soviets in the form of religious guarantees, in exchange for the avalanche of American help about to flow into Russia in convoy after convoy?

As it later developed, the efforts (Braun's) made to convince the American mission of the supreme opportunity of the moment do not seem to have met with any great success. Mr. Harriman barely had time to listen to what was being told him.

It was almost as though Harriman was afraid that Stalin might refuse Lend-Lease on such a condition. The only public Soviet reaction to the discussion was a statement reported by *Pravda* of October 5 of the assistant director of the Soviet Information Bureau, Lozovsky, who welcomed Roosevelt's words and said they precisely indicated the principles of the Constitution of the USSR on the question of the freedom of religious worship by Soviet citizens. In reply to a further question, Lozovsky said the uproar on religion was "much ado about nothing". Coming only few days after Taylor's optimistic assurances to the Pope on the future of religion in the USSR, such words did nothing to tranquilize the Vatican.

Lozovsky was echoed some time later in London, where the Soviet ambassador, Alexander Maisky, gave a glowing account on the extent of religious freedom in his country. Among the resulting caustic comments was that of the Reverend John Heenan, a well-known radio preacher and later to become cardinal and archbishop of Westminster: "The surest way to cool the ardor of Catholic help to Russia is for Soviet officials to pretend that their record is one of Christian endeavor." The deeply skeptical Braun himself wrote further:

> In a talk with this writer, the American ambassador [Steinhardt] said that an effort had been made to obtain from the Soviet government a declaration on religion which would at the same time satisfy public opinion back home and save Soviet face. The ambassador admitted that this Lozovsky statement was a very poor and unsatisfactory result, adding that was all that could be expected of the Soviets.

Despite the apparent initial stonewalling by the Soviets, changes began to appear. One of the first signs was the early disappearance of the godless newspaper *Bezbozhnik* "because of a shortage of paper". Anti-God museums were discreetly closed "for repairs". On July 19, the *Tablet* (London) noted that the Soviet radio was now (for foreign listeners only) denouncing religious persecution in the German Reich. To the surprise of observers, *Pravda* of

September 3 published excerpts of President Roosevelt's radio address, which included a statement on religion. Even more surprisingly, the same newspaper, on September 8, on the front page, said, "The barbarous fascist hordes, drunk with blood, turn to ridicule the religious sentiments of women—Catholic and Protestant—desecrating churches and violating the sacred vessels."

The radio also gave attention to religious matters. At an early stage the BBC (London) was allowed to broadcast a religious service from Moscow. There was even a "Christian radio station" in German, Polish, Hungarian, and Slovak. These were "clandestine" transmissions, but they were prepared by Comintern personnel. They concluded with the exhortation, "Be ye strong in the battle against the anti-Christ." The approach was generally to dwell on the anti-Christian nature of National Socialism. Call it cynical propaganda, if you will, but it reflected also the anguish of the Russian population in a very desperate hour. The Nazi forces were closing in on Moscow. There was need to bolster the popular will to resist, and mere political commissars were not enough. In these circumstances, traditional antireligious slogans were out of place, even in Stalin's eyes. That explains why in Moscow the radio announced to the surprised public, on the eve of Easter 1942, which fell on April 4, that the usual curfew in the besieged city would be suspended so that the people could attend the traditional midnight Easter liturgy. In itself this concession was little enough. How many churches were open? If the gesture had been omitted, no one would have noticed it. But it was a giant step for the regime as far as the faithful were concerned.

Another factor that undoubtedly had its part to play in the permissiveness in religious matters now in evidence was the attitude of some Orthodox bishops in the areas overrun by the Wehrmacht. In the Ukraine, in White Russia, and in the Baltics, Orthodox bishops welcomed the Germans as liberators. One particular case was the defection of the Exarch Sergei (Voskressensky) of Riga. He was a Moscow appointee, but with German support he carried on successful religious work in occupied

Russia. Stalin was no longer in a position, at least for the moment, to meet religious problems with the method of suppression.

Thus, by October the cause of religion was ranged on both sides of the conflict. While the Italians and the Spanish preached the "crusade", the British and the Americans engaged the Soviet Union on the side of Christianity. On Myron Taylor's return to Washington in early October he stated that the religious issue of the war would be clarified as a result of his visit to the Pope. Only after the war was it learned that he referred to the vexing problem of the papal encyclical of 1937 against cooperating with Communism. On October 6, under the headline "Vatican in Touch with Moscow", the London *News Chronicle* said that Taylor's expedition pointed to the "consolidation of the Christian front against Nazism throughout the world". The Vatican had not, of course, been "in touch" with Moscow. This was hyperbole no doubt permitted to a newspaper in time of war. You could believe it if you wanted to. As usual in wartime, God himself was conscripted too.

It was awkward for the Soviets to make a religious issue out of the Nazi invasion, but the pressures to do so were great. In a very long documentation sent to friendly governments on April 30, 1942, and published, for example, in *Red Star* and *Soviet War News,* Molotov wrote on German atrocities, including the maltreatment of priests in Ukraine and White Russia. He also mentioned a Nazi document that the Red Army had seized in March 1942. This was a study signed by one Lieutenant General Wolfgang Weigand with the title "Current Tasks in the Occupied Regions" and dated October 31, 1941. The signer was the inspector for economic matters on the central front (*Mitte*). Weigand (also known as Weigang) represented the armaments industry, and he recommended the deportation of several million Russians to work in Germany to relieve the manpower shortage.

In his use of the Weigand paper, Molotov left out a large and revealing part, the section: "The Solution of the Church Question in the Occupied Eastern Territories". This was left to others. The well-known writer and Stalin propagandist Ilya Ehrenburg cited it briefly in a domestic radio broadcast on July 19: "The German general Weigand in a report I now quote demands the eradication of Christianity in Russia as a religion unsuited to the people." Even Ehrenburg was not telling the whole story. He did not, and also could not, as a Jew, explain to his listeners that Christianity, according to Weigand, was not suited to the people because it was "infected" by its Jewish roots. The Weigand document recognized that there had been a revival of religion, but it was argued that it had to be channeled. Some kind of religion was needed but not one inherited from Judaism. For that reason, a new kind of clergy had to be created who would preach a Jew-free faith: "It is therefore urgently necessary to prevent the priests [*Popen*] from having any influence in the confessional sense, and at the same time it is necessary to send into the field, as soon as possible, a new class of clergy [*ein neuer Predigerstand*], which after an appropriate if brief formation is able to interpret a Jew-free religion to the population." The Weigand vision, though never put into practice in Russia, speaks eloquently of the ideological intent of the Nazi invaders. For reasons of their own, the Soviet leaders found it inexpedient to make an issue of it. They were satisfied to transmit the full Nazi text to friendly embassies as a confidential document.

Chapter 5

"THE TRUTH ABOUT RELIGION IN RUSSIA"

The Orthodox Church in Russia—and not the Church of Rome—
was the prime target and the first victim of the Bolsheviks. This
drama, perhaps never too well understood, must be read in the
context of Russian tradition. The Patriarchate of Moscow had
always lived under the protection, or, better, control, of the
Czars. There had never been, in Orthodoxy, a classic conflict
between Emperor and Papacy. In the Byzantine world, the civil
power assumed wide-ranging prerogatives in religious matters,
certainly at least in their external aspects. Caesar took unto
himself the lion's share. How does a church with the experience
of Caesaropapism respond to attempts on its apostolic mission?
The fall of Czardom was profoundly disorienting for the simple
believer and even more so for the bishops, leaderless, cast adrift,
and bereft of experience.

The new regime openly and radically departed from the religious traditions once incorporated in Czarism. Apologists of the
new order after 1917, in France, for instance, could brush off the
blasphemous antireligious propaganda as simply normal, if excessive, defense against reactionaries and saboteurs. The Bolsheviks
themselves were more honest. From the first, and increasingly,
Communism revealed itself as waging war not on some political op-
ponent but on religious belief as such, on God. Never, since Julian
the Apostate, had the civil power so openly and persistently, over
such a long period, ranged itself against the religion of a people.

Lenin and, after him Stalin were not willing or able to
destroy the Orthodox Church itself, directly. Some say they

48

thought that Christianity would evaporate of itself under the influence of "scientific knowledge". Even if that were the case, the Bolshevik leaders took every possible means to hasten this supposed destiny. Anti-church assaults there were in abundance: bishops and priests sent to Siberia or shot, with or without trial; churches closed and turned maliciously into atheist museums; privileged opportunities for agitators to attack "superstition" in the school or the press with the crudest and most vulgar caricatures. It became a crime to give religious instruction to children under sixteen years of age. The Patriarchate of Moscow itself was left without a titular for years.

But against all odds, a minimal structure remained in place throughout this calamitous period. Church life continued, if within a very narrow limit. Bishops were consecrated, priests ordained; the liturgy could be celebrated at least on the great feastdays; most of all, the religious sense of the Russian people resisted interiorly. Pious mothers saw to it that their children were baptized, in secret, naturally. The embers never died out but were ready to burst out again in flame. The ambitious and impious Bolshevik campaign, after fifty years of intensive effort in which the state had all the cards, was a monumental failure. It was Bolshevism and not Christianity that "evaporated".

Hitler's war on the Soviet Union in 1941 had a catalytic effect on the religious problem in the Orthodox world. One should not look for a unified pattern. On the contrary, as a corollary to its dependence on the civil power, Orthodoxy was determined more than ever by nationality. The various churches were independent of each other, even among those who recognized the Patriarch of Moscow. In Ukraine, in White Russia, in the Baltics, in Poland, in Rumania and Bulgaria and Finland, Orthodoxy presented many contrasting aspects. The Nazi occupants exploited this vulnerability, supporting independent and diversionist church movements wherever they could. They succeeded in finding bishops ready, for a variety of reasons, to lend themselves to being manipulated in this way.

Among Russians abroad patriotic and national sentiments rose to a high in the face of the critical events in the homeland. What are we to say of the "Synod of Bishops of the Russian Orthodox Churches outside of Russia"? This was a body of Russian Orthodox that established itself between the wars at Karlovcy in Yugoslavia (Serbia). As its name tells us, it gathered survivors and sympathizers of the old church of Czarist times. They were monarchists. The war in their native country could not leave them indifferent. But in which sense? The first instinct was to welcome what appeared to be an imminent liberation of their country by the Germans. In the interwar years, the Karlovcy Synod had good relations with Germany, where so many exiles had found refuge. The Reich government even contributed, in an anti-Bolshevik gesture, to the construction or restoration of the Russian Orthodox cathedral in Berlin in 1938. The Synod's representative in that city was Seraphim (Lade), who had the title "Archbishop of Berlin and of Germany".

An ambiguous situation arose. The Nazis did not trust the potentially dangerous Synod. Karlovcy would inevitably push for the restoration of the Czars, an eventuality far from Nazi intentions. Yet in Berlin, Archbishop Seraphim (who was a German, not a Russian) in the first days issued a call to his people in enthusiastic support of the Nazi war: "A crusade has begun in truth in the name of the salvation of peoples from the forces opposed to Christ. We have awaited this day for more than twenty tormented years." The German army, he said, interpreting an official announcement to his own satisfaction,

> is not fighting against our people but only against that power that has raised persecution against the Church and against the Faith, which profaned, destroyed, and annihilated our holy places, which has transformed our Patria into an object of derision before all the nations, which has poisoned the soul of the people with its planned, diabolical, antireligious, and Communist propaganda, and which seeks in the end to transform the entire world into a Golgotha, into a dungeon, into a kingdom of slaves.

Seraphim's sentiments were no doubt shared by many in Karlovcy. But the Synod never got the confidence of the Nazis. After the war the "Synod of Orthodox Russian Bishops outside of Russia" transferred its center to New York, still dedicated to the restoration of Czarism.

If Karlovcy did not fit into Nazi plans, Berlin found a valuable asset in the cooperation of Exarch Sergei (Voskressensky), already mentioned, in the Baltics. He had been sent to Riga with the invading Red Army in 1940 by his patron, Metropolitan Sergei of Moscow. His work with the Germans after 1941 was therefore treasonable in the view of his superiors in Moscow, though he never broke canonically with the Patriarchate. Sergei was valuable for the Germans in that his defection to their support was a wedge in the enemy ranks. His real state of mind or his real intentions are something of a mystery, as are also the instigators of his violent death. Whose side was he really on? He was strongly anti-Bolshevik, but his work for the revival of religious life in the Soviet Union was not what the Nazis were ready for, over a long period. Besides, could they really trust him? Writers blame the Gestapo, disillusioned or betrayed by him. Others say his liquidation was an act of vengeance on the part of Russian partisans working for the Kremlin secret service. Both hypotheses are plausible, but the second seems much more likely. An important act of Sergei a few weeks earlier throws light on the episode. On April 5, 1944, the exarch had convoked a meeting of bishops and leading priests of the Baltics to Riga, where they issued a strong and lengthy anti-Bolshevik statement warning, in short, that if the Soviets returned it would be the end of the culture of the Baltic peoples. The Riga declaration was greeted with enthusiasm by the German officials and given the widest possible publicity. In sending this long text (six pages, single spaced) to Gestapo chiefs and the Foreign Ministry on April 7, Gestapo chief Ernst Kaltenbrunner added that the exarch had recorded the declaration on a disk and that it would be put on the radio. Wrote Kaltenbrunner further, "I consider the resolution to be adequate and propagandistically serviceable." A few weeks later, on April 30, the exarch was found dead, his body riddled with bullets. Coming on the heels of the April 5 appeal, this strongly suggests that his death was the work of Bolsheviks, who had all the visible provocations they needed.

Sergei had the title of Metropolitan of Lithuania and Vilna and Exarch of Latvia and Estonia. In his previous assignment in the church chancery of Moscow he had frequent contacts with the Soviet police—a task he carried out with so much skill that he was suspected of being a police agent. He had not left Riga when the Soviets evacuated the city in 1941, hiding in the crypt of his cathedral. At least that is what he told the Germans. He displayed the same ambiguous gift when dealing with the Nazi occupants. The Germans saw in Sergei the way to penetrate Russia through the Russian Orthodox Church. He was still under the obedience of the Moscow Patriarchate. The exarch, when expressing his opinion of a conference of Orthodox bishops held in Vienna in October 1943, which challenged the legitimacy of the election of the new Patriarch, was careful to say in the German-controlled press on November 7 that he could not comment on the Vienna resolution without having the exact text before him. He commented, however, that the Vienna delegates were all "schismatics" and it was not their right to pronounce on the validity of the election. As far as he was concerned, the restoration of the Patriarchate was a sign of weakness on Stalin's part.

Pastorally Sergei was energetic and successful, perhaps because of the large number of Russians in his jurisdiction, refugees or not. From the earliest days of the Nazi penetration into Russia, he had initiated the sending of priests over the border. His efforts were centered on the ancient monastery of Pechorsky, near Pskov. The "Mission", as it was called, was an immediate success, being heartily welcomed by the population. In a year it had grown to seventy priests—Orthodox Russians brought from the Baltics, all of them anti-Bolshevik but loyal to the Moscow Patriarchate— ministering to two hundred parishes. The restored monastery of Pskov became a beehive of activity, for example, in the preparation of liturgical items in such short supply after years of persecution.

The Reich government approved all this. According to a report to Alfred Rosenberg from Reichskommissar Hinrich Lohse in Riga on June 27, 1942, Sergei had been told, "There are no objections against the Orthodox mission in the old Soviet area, which he had already undertaken around Pskov right after the coming of the German troops and before the creation of the German civil organization in Riga, with the approval of the SD [Security Services]." The same report to Rosenberg paid tribute to Sergei for having already achieved "great anti-Bolshevik propaganda successes" in the church sector and beyond. The thinking of Sergei and his Nazi sponsors was that as adherents of the Patriarchate his anti-Bolshevik priests would be acceptable to the Russian faithful as canonically legitimate and not as emissaries of a foreign power.

But by the middle of 1943 the Nazi officials were receiving reports of partisans infiltrating this work, ostentatiously showing themselves favorable to religion. In fact, partisan leaders were said to have actually ordered the dubious and fearful local faithful to attend church services. They obviously had their orders. Some of the priests, it was also said, did not believe what they saw and decamped with their families. With the deteriorating military situation, Sergei's ideas were beginning to backfire. Were his own priests joining the partisans?

There was a third way of reacting to Bolshevism in Russia: surrender. This was the course pursued by the Patriarchate itself. The Synod of Karlovcy referred to earlier saw the solution in the restoration of the Romanovs. Exarch Sergei of Riga envisaged absolute resistance to the entire Bolshevik system of government. The Patriarchate arrived at open submission of the Orthodox Church to the Soviet regime. Recognition of the legitimacy of the Soviet regime meant equivalently attributing to Stalin the same prerogatives that the Czars had enjoyed in respect to the Church: that is, subjection—far more pronounced than had ever been seen in Czarist times. This is the explanation for the notorious propaganda book issued in the name of Metropolitan Sergei of Moscow under the title *The Truth about Religion in Russia* appearing in a limited edition for export in June 1942. The Soviets had already often asserted that religion was free, that there was "no persecution", and so on. But they felt it necessary to reaffirm this in a more striking way for world opinion. This was to have the Moscow Patriarchate itself sponsor a long apologia in this sense. The Moscow church leaders were ready, in those cataclysmic war years, to oblige. We can quote the entire first paragraph of the preface of Metropolitan Sergei as "guardian of the patriarchal throne", which nails down his principles and his scope:

> This book, first of all, is an answer to the Fascist "crusade" undertaken by them, as it were, for the sake of "liberating" our people and our Orthodox Church from the Bolsheviks. But along with this the book answers the general question: Does our Church admit that it is being persecuted by the Bolsheviks, and does it ask anyone to liberate it from such persecution?

With these words Sergei bravely reasserted that there was "no persecution"—the imputation that perpetually harassed the regime—and that it repudiated "rescue" efforts from abroad, meaning, above all, Orthodox critics, such as the Karlovcy Synod. No mention is made of existing antireligious legislation or official pronouncements on religion. Stalin's name is never mentioned. Even the question of persecution raised by Sergei is never faced. Loyalty to the regime is emphasized as if it were the only question with which the Orthodox Church was concerned. The silences and omissions were all too eloquent.

The book appeared in a deluxe edition with numerous photographs of Russian religious life. It carried various earlier statements of the acting Patriarch, Metropolitan Sergei of Moscow, with quotations from Metropolitan Nikolai of Kiev and Galicia (successor of Exarch Sergei in the chancery) and other Church spokesmen. An appendix presented testimonials of the faithful about their sufferings under the German occupation.

A long study of *The Truth about Religion in Russia* prepared as of January 6, 1944, by the Research and Analysis Branch of the American Office of Strategic Services (OSS) observed, "Evidence of this sort should be of value in combating German claims that they are fighting for Christian Europe against the barbarous and godless Russians." The OSS analysis concluded:

> The fact that a religious book of this nature was published in the USSR in 1942 (by permission, if not by inspiration, of the government) is of considerable significance, especially when it is remembered that religious publication in the Soviet Union ceased in 1929, whereas anti-religious propaganda was continued until the German invasion in June 1941. This book is proof that the Soviet government is willing to enjoy the cooperation of the Russian Church against the Nazis. A *modus vivendi* between the two authorities is thus shown to be possible. On the other hand there is nothing in his book to guarantee that an anti-religious attitude will not again be assumed by the Soviet government after the war, although at present this development seems improbable.

The OSS paper of 1944 reflected the wishful thinking prevailing in Allied circles at that point of the war as regards the future course of Josef Stalin in the spirit of the Atlantic Charter. It would have been out of place for the OSS to observe wickedly that now it had become the turn for the Bolsheviks, too, to claim to be "fighting for Christian Europe", after decades of anti-God measures.

On the face of it *The Truth* was attention drawing for several reasons. First, it was the first religious book that the government allowed to be printed for years. As such, it stood out like the proverbial sore thumb. Was it not bizarre to find a book extolling the "freedom" of the Church that itself was the first of its kind to appear in ages? Second, it was *not* available to the Russians in Moscow. The entire edition was meant for export, for open defense propaganda, mostly to be distributed gratis to governments and specialists in the media.

As for the contents, critics abroad, especially Russian exiles, found it easy to point out glaring and revealing omissions and silences in a book with such a title. An easy target was the preface of Metropolitan Sergei. It was almost as if the writer were trying to send a signal to the world by practically inviting attention to the real situation of the Church under the Bolsheviks. (Can we absolutely exclude such an intention on Sergei's part, paradoxical but feasible considering the subtleties of existence in the Orthodox world of those years?)

Would it be better not to probe further into the mind of the future Patriarch of Moscow? The times were out of joint. Was this the price Sergei had to pay for the reconstitution of the Patriarchate, which occurred in the spring of 1943? How far did Sergei represent authentic Orthodox theological thinking?

Sergei was not following the courageous example of his predecessor, Patriarch Tykhon, who died in 1925. Much, of course, happened in the succeeding years. Even with his experience of Caesaropapism, Tykhon made strong resistance to the Bolsheviks in defense of the Church, for which he paid a heavy personal price. He was accused by the Bolsheviks of serving only Czarism, not the cause of religion. If that accusation had any validity, what can be said of the opportunism of Sergei in the face of the Bolsheviks? The most benevolent interpretation of Sergei at the time was that he had retreated to the inner religious life, even if that meant humiliating betrayal of tradition.

Some mortified coreligionists at that time suggested that Sergei's submission to Stalin in such an abject form was not opportunism but rather the fruit of a profound conviction that for the sake of remaining with the people the Church had to go into the abyss and give up everything, including its dignity and its honor. This road of self-abnegation, it was said, was inspired by the belief in the all-conquering power of Jesus Christ. That is, nothing really matters so long as people are allowed to worship him and to hear his Gospel read at the services and to be assisted in their daily life by the sacraments of the Church.

Such a highly mystical interpretation was uttered in Orthodox circles in London, outside of Russia, in order to make sense out of what they had to contemplate. They had to admit that their vision did not coincide with traditions of Christians of the West.

Chapter 6

FASCIST PRESSURE ON THE VATICAN

The task of getting Vatican moral support for the "anti-Bolshevik war" fell to Fascist Italy. The Nazi Reich was absent, for its own reasons. The targets were twofold: the bishops themselves and the Pope. The Italy of Mussolini was destined to be disappointed in both respects. In 1940, the Fascist press already had to lament that the Italian hierarchy, unlike their opposite numbers in enemy countries, did not rally around their government with express pledges of approval and support. This was a frequent reproach of Roberto Farinacci, director of *Il Regime Fascista* of Cremona.

In mid-August 1941 this newspaper complained that the faithful had been without guidance since June. "Catholics", Farinacci wrote piously, "wish to be given directives in order to know for whom they should pray." On September 13 the *Tablet* (London), in a review of the Italian press, noted that the Fascist press was showing "considerable annoyance" at the lack of any Vatican condemnation of the British and Polish link with the Soviets or of U.S. aid to the Bolsheviks. *Il Messagero* and *Il Regime Fascista,* reported the London journal, were particularly shrill. Said the *Regime Fascista,* "Closely watching the Vatican's tendencies, we fail to discern any atmosphere of hostility to Russia in the Holy See. Above all, *L'Osservatore Romano* continues intrepidly to serve all the allies and friends of Stalin." Fascist newspapers and agencies contributed initially to this campaign by carrying stories, chiefly from their Berlin correspondents, of a religious revival in the newly occupied areas, such as the Ukraine. By the time of the return to Rome of Myron C. Taylor in September, reports of this

kind were still being filed from Berlin—eventually fading out in
the face of the realities of Nazi occupation policy. Some specimens from *Il Messagero* follow.

On September 15, it carried a Stefani agency story from Berlin
on Lithuania. The new Reichskommissar, Hinrich Lohse, was
said to have had cordial meetings with Church leaders in which
he assured them of his desire to help in every way. The irony of
this alleged readiness escaped Stefani completely. Lohse was an
intimate collaborator of Alfred Rosenberg, author of *The Myth of
the Twentieth Century*. His presence in Catholic Lithuania should
have been a warning. On the twenty-fourth the same agency said
that religious life was resuming in such newly occupied cities as
Smolensk and Borisov. On the twenty-sixth it said, still from
Berlin, that four Ukrainian bishops (Orthodox) had thanked
Hitler for liberating the Church from the Bolsheviks. Italian
Catholic papers themselves carried accounts from chaplains describing the revival of religious sentiment in Russia.

Could the Italian reader not wonder why the Pope did not
seem enchanted with such happy events?

It was indeed difficult for Ambassador Attolico to satisfy the
expectations of his superiors. In a report of August 2, addressing
himself not only to his immediate superiors in the Foreign Ministry but also to the Ministry of Popular Culture (Propaganda), he
reacted to the disappointment. Germany was the problem:

> The ministry will have noticed the reluctance of the Vatican to
> take a position on the political plane in favor of Germany in
> the struggle it is conducting against the USSR. Such taking of
> a stand has proved impossible, as the Holy See has reasons to
> criticize Germany for its antireligious policy, a real and proper
> persecution, as we ourselves have been able to experience even
> recently, for example, in Slovenia. And not only that, informa-
> tion reaching us just now from Lisbon tells us: It is estimated
> that three hundred priests have been shot and about a thou-
> sand are dying in prison in the first year of the German
> occupation of Poland. Twenty-seven hundred priests were
> imprisoned, of whom fourteen hundred are still in concentra-

tion camps or in the Austrian salt mines. Those arrested most recently include the bishop of Lodz [Vladimir Jasinski], his coadjutor, and five canons.

In such a situation the Vatican (I say "Vatican" because as for the bishops, for example, the bishop of Gorizia, Monsignor Carlo Margotti, they have been left free to express themselves as they wish) finds itself in the impossibility of calling an anti-Bolshevik crusade; where in fact are the crusaders?

In short, according to Attolico (who had come from the post in Berlin, where he learned at first hand the facts of Nazi anti-Church policy), the "anti-Bolshevik war" could not be considered a bona fide crusade so long as Germany continued its persecution of the Church, inside or outside the Reich.

The ambassador raised the question of Vatican "mutism" with Monsignor Tardini on September 5, if not earlier. On September 16 he spoke directly to Pius XII, on his own initiative — or just as likely on orders from Foreign Minister Count Galeazzi Ciano. If the Pope did not feel able to pronounce on the war in his own name, could he not have some leading bishop in Italy commit the hierarchy to the cause of the "crusade"? The Pontiff seemed at first disposed to adopt this solution, but he did not give an immediate answer. But in a few days the newspapers reported an alleged pastoral of the archbishop of Bologna, Cardinal Giovanni Battista Rocca da Corneliano. *Il Messagero* of September 20 described it as "a vibrant pastoral of Cardinal Nasalli Rocca against Bolshevism".

The Roman newspaper gave a resume of the cardinal's words. He developed how the new hordes of barbarians wished to destroy the kingdom of God and had launched either atheism or paganism:

> We do not want to deny that there has been a marvelous flourishing of energy and spiritual life. But we do not conceal the terrible historical facts of destructive Bolshevism, which has been shown in Spain, and the terrible historical facts of persecution against the Church and its priests which raged in

other countries. Italy, by the grace of God, has remained free from this; all praise to its leaders and to its people.

Cardinal Nasalli Rocca did refer to Nazi persecution with the single word *paganism* —language that in those days meant Nazism. For Pius XII that was too little. But the Bologna story fitted the bill and resolved the Pontiff's perplexity. Only later was it learned that the archbishop had not issued a pastoral but had simply written a letter to a pious Rosary society. Monsignor Tardini wrote, "His Holiness has seen the report of *Il Messagero* and considers that this intervention of the eminent archbishop of Bologna ought to be enough." He had already made up his own mind.

On September 18, Tardini recorded, "His Holiness, after having read the most recent grave news about Germany, told me that it is no longer possible to have a diocesan cardinal speak out against only Bolshevism." In the very weeks of August–September, the Nazis in Bavaria and elsewhere were removing crucifixes from the schools. These were the crusaders against Bolshevism in defense of Christian civilization? Pius XII refused to be drawn into a stultifying position. He had priorities other than the singleminded undiscriminating anti-Communism attributed to him so tendentiously and so ignorantly in later years.

Ambassador Attolico developed his thought more precisely in conversations with Tardini on September 17, the day after his inconclusive audience with the Pope. The war, he said, promised to be long and not a matter of weeks. If the Pope thought it would be over soon and for this reason preferred to keep silent, now that it seemed likely to drag on, perhaps there might be place for "some kind of pronouncement against Communism on the part of Catholics". He argued further that the Italian people, now convinced that the war would continue because of Bolshevism, would like to have "some kind of word from the authorities of the Church". He said he could understand that the Holy Father, in speaking against Communism, would also have to speak at the same time against Germany, and he would prefer then that he did not speak at all. Why could not some Italian prelate outside the Vatican take on the responsibility? In that case, the bishop could easily be seen to speak as an Italian, for the Italian troops, fighting Communism. Would it not be possible to have Catholic Action pass on the word to the parish priests to preach against Communism? In short, the Vatican should issue a "suggestion" or an "encouragement" to the bishops. Attolico commented, perhaps bitterly, that it was too bad the bishops felt themselves tied so closely to the Holy See. This link, he said, echoing an old refrain of Italian politicians, "is not an advantage, politically and nationally, for Italy".

Pius XII was unmovable. A few weeks later, Berlin heard about it from its own embassy in Rome. The account, related by Attolico to the German diplomats, tells of the motives that impelled the Pope to be so adamant. We have Attolico's version of his papal audience, appearing in a dispatch to the Reich Foreign Ministry from the German Vatican embassy:

> While conversing with the Pope I made the point of bringing up the subject of Bolshevism. But the Pope gave me the same reply as that of the cardinal secretary of state [Maglione] and his assistants [Tardini and Montini], although with greater emphasis and assuredness. The Holy See, said the Pope, has already spoken out, in good time, that is, on Bolshevism and has *never* (in text) changed. If anything, it is the others who have changed. Germany was the first to make every effort to get along with Bolshevism, not the Holy See.

Attolico went on to cite the Pope's own words:

> But if I should talk of Bolshevism, and I would be fully prepared to do so, continued the Pope, should I say nothing of Nazism? The situation in Germany, he told me, has become infinitely worse since my own departure from Berlin. Even if the Führer has ordered the "suspension" of the persecutions, this does not mean that Christ has been readmitted to the schools from which he was removed, and that the numerous convents and religious institutions now closed will be reopened, or that the German children will no longer be made to recite that parody of the Our Father in which they thank Hitler for their daily bread.

This was strong language from one known to weigh his words. Dr. Bernardo Attolico, ex-ambassador of Italy to Berlin, recalled by Mussolini for his lack of sympathy for the Axis ally, was probably well pleased to bring this unpleasant information to his German colleague in the Vatican from the mouth of Pius XII.

Were the Italian bishops individually so "mute" about the issues of the war, before or after 1941? The *Regime Fascista* of Roberto Farinacci was extremist even by Fascist standards, and it was waging its own war on the Vatican and *L'Osservatore Romano*. Attolico made it his business to cull from the newspapers whatever patriotic sentiments he could find. He reported in August, "All things considered, therefore, the point has been reached when it can no longer be said that the Holy See has not taken a position in the struggle against Bolshevism. It has done so, but in the Vatican style, that is, with the moderation and caution proper to the Vatican's mission." He reported again as late as September 11, "I believe I can assert that today the whole Italian Catholic world is ranged compactly with the regime in the struggle against Bolshevism." Such confidence was a bit premature, as is proved by Attolico's about-face in a few days when he went to the Pope asking for something more. Why were these scattered references he collected and sent to the Ministry no longer convincing?

There was indeed no lack of patriotism among the bishops, ardently in support of the "crusade". One of the most explicit protagonists of the "anti-Bolshevik war" was the bishop of Gorizia, Carlo Margotti, already mentioned by Attolico, who could not have pleased the government more. In a pastoral of July 16 he called for prayers for the Axis victory over Russia and compared the campaign to the ancient Christian Crusades for the Faith:

> Just as in times past the venerable hierarchy of the Church blessed the volunteer militia, departing from the West to liberate the Holy Sepulchre of Christ profaned, so also, today, we salute and we bless the Legionaries of Italy who ready themselves and their allies in a common effort to open the immense prison that has held the Russian populations, depriving them of their right to believe and to profess their Faith freely.

The Legionaries, went on the bishop of Gorizia, would save both civilization and the Faith. No other diocesan bishop distinguished himself with such a dramatic religious appeal. But others issued prayers for "victory" without drawing too close a parallel with ancient times.

If such episcopal statements pleased the government at the time, discontent set in. By the beginning of 1942, voices were still heard criticizing Italian Catholics for their "mutism". The minister of the interior, Guido Buffarini-Guidi, in the first days of January observed to the papal nuncio, Francesco Borgongini Duca, that while the archbishop of New York, Francis Spellman, had sent a message of support to President Roosevelt (after the Pearl Harbor attack) in the name of the U.S. bishops and all U.S. Catholics, in Italy the Catholic episcopate could not do likewise. But the most significant sign of Fascist chagrin appeared in the pages of the Fascist review, *Critica Fascista,* of February 15, with an editorial signed "Civis", the pen name of the editor, Giuseppe Bottai. The occasion was the anniversary of the Lateran pacts of 1929, which marked the reconciliation of the Holy See with Italy. The writer lamented that the Holy See had not preached the crusade against Bolshevism. Clear words were still wanting: "We expected it. We thought it inevitable—because never in history has the Church had an enemy more fearful than Bolshevism." Instead, said the review, when the war broke out in Russia, it even looked as if the fight between the Church and her worst enemy had disappeared. What was more, "when the paralytic liar in the White House announced that the heart of Stalin was consumed by the same fire of Divine Love that transformed Saint Teresa, no one saw astonishment change to outrage, indignation, at this unheard-of falsehood." The editorial went on, "In the moment when the state, which had sanctioned in the solemn Lateran pact 'the sovereignty of the Holy See in the international field, as an inherent attribute of its nature', declared war on that state which for years fought against Christianity, the Christians are silent."

As far as the Italian government could see, someone was putting the brake on Italian Catholic opinion. In view of the numerous episcopal prayers for victory, in view of the diligent efforts of the Military Ordinariate to provide moral and material support to the soldiers in the field, the dissatisfaction on the part of regime can be puzzling. But there is really no mystery. The real complaint was not that the bishops were neglecting their patriotic duty but that the Pope himself was failing to give his support to the "anti-Bolshevik crusade".

Chapter 7

THE "CRUSADE" AS SEEN
BY THE GERMAN BISHOPS

When the Nazi attack on the Soviet Union opened, the U.S. chargé at the Vatican, Harold H. Tittman, Jr., asked Monsignor Montini on June 28 whether the report was true that the German Catholic bishops had issued a pastoral letter against Bolshevism and whether the Vatican had had any part in it. In other words, was the Holy See backing the Nazi war on the Soviet Union? This query was prompted by the completely fabricated DNB (German News Agency) story already mentioned, which appeared also in the Italian press. Montini, substitute secretary of state, replied that he had no information of such a pastoral and if any existed the Vatican had nothing to do with it.

Tittman's query and the answer lead us to the question of German Catholic support of the 1941 events and the attitude of the Holy See toward their stand. The correspondence of the Vatican with the German bishops at this period is conspicuous for complete silence on the subject. In his numerous letters to the German bishops individually or collectively, Pope Pius XII never mentioned the Russian war. Since these were confidential letters to prelates whom he knew personally, the Pope might have been expected to reveal his thoughts on the "crusade" if he really believed the extension of war to the East deserved such a description. Instead, the only mention of Russia occurred when the Pontiff complained of the obstacles put in his path by the Reich government in his efforts to communicate news of war prisoners in Russia. He lamented that he would have been able to do more if the Soviet and German governments had been willing to use the Holy See as an intermediary. One can conclude from this that the German bishops never asked for explicit or implicit guidelines on what should be their stand, and likewise that the Pope felt no compulsion to give any. The secretariat of state, for its part, did not reveal its mind to the nuncio on this aspect of the war or suggest to him how the bishops should conduct themselves. The only hint of anything along this line is found in a report of October 4 from Nuncio Orsenigo, who said that "fortunately" (his words) some of the bishops at least had come out in support of the war against Russia. He referred especially to the September 14 message of Bishop von Galen of Münster, about which more below. In making this remark, Orsenigo gave expression to his personal fear that the German bishops were making a serious mistake in not being more patriotic in their public utterances. Whether Germany won or lost the war, he anticipated, it would be held against the Church that her leaders had failed the nation in the hour of mortal crisis. The nuncio spoke for himself, and there is no sign in the documentation that the Pope differed from the bishops.

The preoccupation of both the Holy See and the German bishops at mid-1941 was not Bolshevism but the pressing near-disastrous condition of the Church in Germany. Even Orsenigo in these days was far busier bringing protests to the Foreign Ministry than in urging the bishops to be more patriotic. The new phase of the war was accompanied by more revealing anti-Church measures in occupied Poland, above all in that part of Poland closest to Germany and annexed directly to the Reich. This zone, renamed the Warthegau (largest center Posen, or Poznan), was intended to be the proving ground or model for the future Nazi state according to plans worked out by party ideologues.

Berlin's first war communiques were uniformly optimistic and pointed to yet another Blitzkrieg. On October 9, the press officer of the Reichschancellery, Otto Dietrich, stated categorically, "The campaign against Russia is concluded; the military decision is definitive." Who could stop the Führer? Anyone could easily anticipate that the next victim would be the churches, Catholic

and Protestant, in Germany itself. It is with this background of
apprehension for the future that the ensuing episcopal statements
are to be considered. The annual conference of the German
bishops was about to assemble at Fulda when the news came of
the new front in Russia. The conference already had in preparation a vigorous statement of protest and alarm over the anti-
Church restrictions of the government, and, despite the new
developments, they went ahead with it as if nothing had happened.
Their letter was issued under date of June 26 and was entirely
devoted to the state of the Church. There was no mention of the
war on Russia. On July 16 Cardinal Adolf Bertram of Breslau, as
president of the conference, transmitted detailed complaints of
the bishops to Hanns Kerrl, head of the Reich Ministry of Ecclesiastical Affairs. Bertram was rewarded with a blanket rejection of
everything along with a lecture on the failure of the bishops to
rise to their patriotic duties. On August 4 Kerrl wrote:

> On June 22 the Führer informed the world public that the
> German nation in the interest of all humanity has entered into
> a struggle against its most dangerous and most strongly armed
> enemy. From a conference of *German* [in text] bishops which
> met from June 24 to June 26, we could have expected that in
> these days the great fact that the German nation has entered
> into battle against the enemy of mankind, which persecutes
> not only the Christian Church but religion itself with fanatical
> fury, would have inflamed the zeal of the bishops and filled
> them with the one desire to employ all their strength so that
> the faithful under their influence should be inspired with
> confidence in victory. The Fulda bishops, on the contrary,
> were not apparently interested in these concerns of all Ger-
> mans today. German bishops considered it much more neces-
> sary at this very time to send to those over whom they think
> they have some influence a pastoral letter that is certainly not
> filled with the desire to strengthen confidence in the leader-
> ship of the German people but rather to shake it.

Kerrl's communication must have been written more for the
attention of his Nazi superiors than for the bishops. What else, in

fact, could he reply to the complaints? He took the stance of pretending that no persecution existed. He was not the first Reich agency to complain of the negative attitude of the Church leaders. In the first months of the war the Propaganda Ministry summoned Catholic representatives for a dressing down. They were reproached for their "defeatism" and lack of enthusiasm for the war cause. This rebuke must have been perplexing to the bishops. They had been given to understand that the Reich did not need their support and they should restrain themselves while the nation pursued its course. Moreover, the bishops were explicitly told, during this short-lived armistice of the Soviet-Nazi pact, to cease their criticisms of the Soviet Union. Now they were being reprimanded for not being zealous enough in the fight against "Germany's greatest enemy". In reality, Hitler and the party leaders did not at all want the Catholic bishops to speak out on the war, before or after 1941. They did not want any "help". The Church was not to get any credit for helping to win the war. Two brilliant Blitzkriegs had built up an enormous confidence in themselves. They were not concerned with the bishops' support— or even world support, for that matter. Besides, even if the bishops had spoken out differently, the Goebbels-controlled press and radio would not have publicized it. When later some bishops did give sermons in the "patriotic sense", Goebbels did not print them. In that way it would be easy, after the victorious campaign, to accuse and crush the Catholic Church for having failed in her duty—in short, for having stabbed Germany in the back.

A reply to Kerrl was in fact prepared, but it was not sent. Did Minister Kerrl really expect, or deserve, an answer? However, the draft provides illuminating insight into the mind of the bishops. The project made the point that there was no need for a new call against godless Bolshevism. They had already, with other pastorals in the past, emphasized the Bolshevik danger, specifically, in 1921, 1924, 1933, and 1936. (It was a regular Nazi theme in the early years that Hitler had saved the Church from a Bolshevik takeover or, in reverse at other moments, that the Church was conspiring with the Bolsheviks—both allegations always vehemently denied.) The draft went on with biting irony:

> Our attitude did not change when after the Russian treaty [1939] the Reich government through the Ministry of Ecclesiastical Affairs and through the Reich press office prohibited references to Communism and Bolshevism in Church bulletins and magazines.

As for the criticisms of the Reich leadership, that is, of Hitler and his aides, it was their duty, they said—or proposed to say—to seek the reasons why confidence was already wavering in wide sectors of the population.

> We do not make any complaints over the sacrifices and restrictions the war requires; the war found us and still finds us everywhere ready to fulfill the same duties that weigh on everyone. But we cannot be silent; the war does not find us all as men with equal rights. We are threatened and oppressed by attitudes that often seem interchangeable with the mentality of Bolshevism. It finds us threatened and oppressed by facts that often take all inner meaning and inner justification out of the fight against Bolshevism.

It was not until three months after the new phase of the war that some patriotic voices began to be raised on the subject. Surprisingly, the most conspicuous if not the first utterance was that of Bishop Clemens von Galen of Münster. His sermons on the Nazis' persecution and especially against the killing of the "useless" (euthanasia) had aroused world attention earlier that year as well as stirring the party to fury. The British propaganda services energetically saw to it that three pastorals or sermons became widely known and commented on. But the same services did not, be it said, take similar notice of a fourth message of the "Lion of Münster". It is easy to understand why. In a pastoral letter, dated September 14 but read in the churches on September 26, Bishop von Galen made his due patriotic pledge of hearty support of the war in the East. But he then spoiled it all, as far as the party —and the British services—was concerned, by raising the invidious comparison of Bolshevism with National Socialism. He declared:

God is my witness that I wish all success, with a warm heart, to the German armies against godless Communism. It is my daily prayer, and I pray daily to God the Lord of Hosts. God is also my witness that it is my love for the German people and my horror of the impious doctrines and crimes of Bolshevism that cause me to point to the danger that threatens behind the victorious German army: the false doctrines and errors that are similar to Russian Communism. In Germany, too, naturalism and materialism are tolerated and encouraged. If there is no stop to this, they will pave the way in our German fatherland for the spiritual domination of Bolshevism of which the Führer spoke on June 22.

The fortunes of Galen's fourth pastoral provide a typical case history of the destiny of Church statements in those times. This was one Galen utterance that the British for once could not afford to make use of: the comparison of Bolshevism with Nazism was too awkward for the British to play up now that the Soviet Union was an ally. The Goebbels-controlled press also passed it over in the usual silence, but party circles fumed and contemplated revenge and reprisals.

On Galen, the confidential publication of the British Foreign Office, *Review of the Foreign Press,* could cite the Belgian paper *Le Soir* of October 31–November 2 but says that nothing was carried in the German newspapers. For foreign consumption, we find carefully screened excerpts in the Bulletin (*Mitteilungen*) of the German legation in Bern of November 1. Hitler's war on Russia, Galen is there reported as saying, was a solution of the problem of Communism, and he is cited as hailing the event. Our duty, he is made to say, is to help our brave soldiers, and also at home our mission is to keep away the ideas and principles that prepared the way for Bolshevism. No mention is made, naturally, of the bishop's linking of National Socialism with Bolshevism.

In Münster, however, where Galen's language was better understood, the party reacted with threats and countermeasures. A Gestapo informant in Düsseldorf (in the diocese of Münster) reported on September 30, two days after:

Bishop Clemens August von Galen on September 28, 1941, had a new pastoral letter read in the churches of his diocese in which he at first takes a stand against Bolshevism and then tries to establish that Bolshevism and National Socialism are fundamentally the same. "It is of no use", he said, "if our brave soldiers overcome Bolshevism militarily, when at the same time through the current efforts in the Reich, Bolshevism gains ground spiritually in our people."

Another report, a week later, from the same Gestapo office:

> In the countryside, especially that which belongs to the diocese of Münster, confessional agitation disturbs the joy over the successes of the German Wehrmacht. The latest pastoral of the bishop of Münster of September 28, 1941, which tries to draw a parallel between Bolshevism and National Socialism, has found its greatest effect in educated Catholic circles. By way of countering the reading of the pastoral letter, the party has organized incessant counterannouncements. After these meetings the question is raised more and more in the population as to why the bishop, if he is really a traitor, is not arrested.

Again only for foreign consumption, the German information services provided other, equally tailored, episcopal quotations in support of the war in Russia. If there were any criticisms or qualifications, implicit or other, in the original, this was not the place to look for them. The *Mitteilungen* of the Bern legation in a following issue, of November 5, mentioned two such statements. The bishop of Augsburg, Joseph Kumpfmüller, on September 22 compared the war in Russia to the battle of Lepanto at which the Turks were defeated by the Christian coalition. Another danger looms, he said, that of the so-called Bolshevism, and he expressed encouragement to the soldiers at the front, saying: "We wish nothing more earnestly than their early definitive victory over the enemies of our Faith." October, Rosary month, instituted by Pope Saint Pius V to commemorate Lepanto, also provided the occasion for similar remarks by the bishop of Regensburg, Michael Buchberger, dated September 24, imploring the intervention of the Virgin Mary for peace—"on our Church today, on our beloved fatherland, and especially on our warriors engaged in heavy fighting against godlessness and inhuman Bolshevism".

There were other such statements by individual bishops not mentioned by the bulletin of the Bern legation. Bishop Michael Rackl of Eichstätt wrote on September 24 that the fight against Russia was "a crusade, a holy war for homeland and people, for Faith and Church, for Christ and his Holy Cross". Further, in a sermon on his installation in October, the new archbishop of Paderborn, Lorenz Jaeger, spoke of the struggle "for the protection of Christianity in our fatherland, for the rescue of the Church from the threat of anti-Christian Bolshevism". Somewhat later, in December, Cardinal Michael Faulhaber of Munich, reacting to the confiscation of church bells, remarked resignedly, "For the dear fatherland we will make this sacrifice also if now it has become necessary for the successful prosecution of the war and for the defeat of Communism."

It is possible that these conspicuously belated patriotic expressions were intended in part as an answer to Hanns Kerrl's complaint, or as an answer to complaints in the Catholic populations that their dear ones on the Soviet front, or indeed themselves on the home front, were entitled to religious consolation amid the hardships that fell on them. The bishops, however, had a right to wonder whether their patriotic urgings served any purpose. Whatever they said was not published in the newspapers. There was by this time no "Catholic press". The pastorals appeared in little diocesan bulletins of small format and often enough only in mimeographed form, not to say circulated clandestinely. The Catholic welfare organization Caritas was forbidden to send religious literature to the troops. It was equally forbidden for pastors to collect the addresses of their own parishioners in the army. In the face of such realities the bishops, whose words were read only in foreign propaganda but censored at home, could have felt themselves exploited in bad faith by National Socialism.

The felt need for patriotic expressions was of short duration. After the bitter winter of 1941–42, a different tone was heard. On

March 20, 1942, the bishops of the Cologne and Paderborn church province issued a pastoral in which there was more protest than patriotism. They contented themselves in their introductory remarks, in the second paragraph, with this statement, which itself implied a rebuke to the regime: "We follow with satisfaction [*Genugtuung*] the fight against the power of Bolshevism, of which the German bishops in numerous pastoral letters had warned German Catholics, whom they had exhorted to vigilance, from 1921 to 1936." But there was no hymn to the fatherland. The rest of the letter is a strong protest against the antireligious measures taken by the regime. The plausibility of the "crusade", if it ever had any, was fading.

The Evangelical (Lutheran) Confession had to face the same division of spirits—to rally patriotically to the fatherland or to face the facts on the home front. One episode of these weeks sets out graphically the doubts and divided counsels the new challenges provoked. The Council for Spiritual Affairs of the German Evangelical Church (DEK) hastened, in the first days, on June 30, to express its solidarity with the regime, addressing Hitler directly with a telegram. It was signed by Dr. August Marahens, Dr. Walter Schultz, and D. Symmen. They saluted the Führer:

> Meeting for the first time since the beginning of the decisive struggle in the East, the Council assures you, once again, our leader, in these exciting and stirring hours, of the unalterable faithfulness and devotion of all Evangelical Christians in the Reich. You, our leader, have banished the Bolshevik danger from our country and now call our nation and the nations of Europe to the decisive onslaught against the deadly enemy of all order and all Western Christian civilization. The German nation, and with it all its Christian members, thank you for this deed.

The telegram also observed that British support of the Soviet Union only proved that it was fighting not really for Christianity but solely for the annihilation of the German people. They prayed for Hitler and the soldiers for a new order which puts "an end to subversion, to blasphemy against God, and to the violations of freedom of conscience". This paean was published at the time, no doubt with astonishment and chagrin, in Switzerland by the Ecumenical Press Service (ICPIS) of the World Council of Churches, edited by the secretary, Visser't Hooft, who also published the absolute dissent that immediately came from Dr. Theophil Wurm, landbishop of Württemberg.

Dr. Wurm wrote to the DEK indignantly that he could not have the telegram read in the churches as requested of him. He said he had urged appropriate prayers but affirmed bluntly, "You have loaded your proclamation with statements of a political content that takes it out of the sphere of a purely church action." He went on acidly:

> No organ of the DEK felt itself obliged to come forward as the defender of Western civilization against Bolshevism when, two years ago, the Soviet treaty of friendship was signed, leading to the handing over of many small countries and peoples to Bolshevism. Certainly every good German is glad that this episode is over and that the German army is executing Europe's reckoning with Communism. But does anyone have the right to speak now who kept silent then?

The bishop also objected to the implication that Hitler was the defender against those who assaulted God and violated freedom of conscience, as though this was the hallmark only of Bolshevism:

> You know as well as I do that a deliberate planned war is being waged in Germany against the Christian education of our youth, against the preaching of the Gospel, against the development of Church life, and against the charitable works of Christianity. You yourselves have been affected by the blows that are being administered against all Christian writings. You have had the same experiences that we have had—that we get no redress from the highest authorities. How then can you express the hope that in the future all this will be no more? Either you should have excluded all these matters from the loyalty pledge in the fight against the external enemy, or, if

you believed that such matters had to be included, then you should have openly spoken of the situation as it really is.

This was a dramatic exposé of the dilemma, on the theoretical and the practical planes, that faced both confessions at this moment in history, in the shadow of the "crusade".

Chapter 8

THE "CRUZADA" IN SPAIN

It was in Spain, more than anywhere else, that the word *crusade* evoked real religious sentiments and was more than a political slogan. The country had just passed through a bitter civil war witnessing acts of violence against the Church and religion under the provocation of Communists supported by Soviet Russia. The word also called up the long struggle, the *Cruzada,* of earlier centuries against the Moors. The Ribbentrop-Molotov pact of August 1939, coming so soon after Franco's definitive victory, was a deep disappointment in Spain (almost as much a shock as the same pact was to so many Communists). Nazi Germany had been a powerful supporter of the new regime, now triumphant in Spain and internationally recognized. The average Spanish Catholic was poorly informed if not misinformed as to the true state of religion under National Socialism. The 1937 anti-Nazi encyclical *Mit brennender Sorge* of Pius XI came at the height of the fighting in Spain, and it was little known in the country even later. In general, papal statements critical of Nazism were played down or censored by the Spanish press. On the contrary, above all after the fall of France in 1940, the prestige of National Socialist Germany reached a new high. The democracies were in retreat; the sympathies of the new Franco government were strongly pro-Reich, all the more since Spain was heavily dependent on Germany for economic reconstruction.

But if the Ribbentrop-Molotov accords of 1939 were disconcerting in Spain, the situation was soon remedied, as much for the Communists as for the Falangists. In June 1941 everything was back in place. The Spain of Generalissimo Francisco Franco rose to the occasion. The imagination caught fire. On June 24, before a massive Falangist rally in Madrid, Foreign Minister Ramon Serrano Suner called on the country to intervene militarily at the side of Germany in the fight against the "red hordes". It was the first move to recruit volunteers for the "Blue Division" (*Division Azul*), to be under the command of General Augustin Muñoz Grandes. By October they were on the Russian front. With replacements it is estimated that a total of forty thousand "volunteers" (there was no declaration of war) passed through this unit. Casualties were heavy until the division was completely withdrawn in 1944.

Inevitable in the "crusade" were tighter relations with National Socialist Germany. Some newspapers went so far as to identify the Reich with the cause of Christianity. *El Alcazar,* one of the worst offenders, for instance, declared that Nazism was "a religious movement founded on the principles of Christianity". The emotion was fueled by mendacious dispatches from Berlin on alleged enthusiastic support by the German bishops. The *El Alcazar* of June 25 carried a Spanish (EFE) agency story on the Nazi-Soviet war under this headline: "Crusade for Christianity". In the EFE story it was stated that the German episcopate had that day "directed a message to all the priests of the German dioceses in which it was declared that the fight against the Soviet Union is a fight for the Christianity of the entire world". In the same letter, the German bishops were said to have "instructed their faithful that it is particularly in the Soviet Union where Christians suffered most cruelly". In these Catholic circles, the EFE story continued, "it is announced that it is possible that the bishops would send a message to the Führer in which they would say that the Catholic Church of Germany would take part, by words and deeds, in the gigantic struggle against Communism."

This "news" from Berlin was an incredible tissue of falsehoods and inventions. The German bishops had not sent any message to the faithful on the subject of the war, and the pastoral they did issue just at this time from Fulda was a blistering protest against the Reich's antireligious policy. No letter was ever sent or intended to be sent to Hitler in support of the war. The EFE story originated in the Berlin propaganda center for readers abroad. Nothing of this sensational information appeared in the press of the Reich. Nevertheless, the barefaced fabrications from Berlin were enough for *El Alcazar* to commit itself to a lyric flight of fancy on the same page:

> The European rallying to the powers that have thrown the weight of their arms against Communism is a unanimous, spontaneous, and mystical solidarity in this war against the common enemy of Christian civilization, which has inflicted on so many decent peoples, together with its subversive principles, in the last twenty years of revolution, blood, and tears in abundance. . . . As if this were not enough, the action of the German clergy and bishops, who raising their voice expressly and clearly to all Christians, recognizes in the present struggle all the transcendence it draws from Christianity and accords to it all the ardor, all the enthusiasm, and all the mysticism worthy of a great and true crusade.

It should be added that the Spanish newspapers were not the only ones taken in by brazenly false Nazi propaganda. The identical (slightly edited) service was sent by the United Press to its subscribers in the United States and appeared, for example, in the *New York Times* of June 25. The UP story stated, "The German Catholic episcopate today sent to all dioceses a message describing the war against Russia as a battle for Christianity all over the world. The clergy was directed to point out in sermons next Sunday that Christianity had been subjected to terrible persecution in Bolshevik Russia." Contradicting itself a few months later, the same United Press service, carried by the *New York Times* of November 11, reported an alleged wave of sermons against Bolshevism. Forgetting what it had already reported in June, the UP gave this enlightening revelation: "It was the first time the Bolshevik theme has been stressed in the German Catholic churches since the start of the war with Russia."

The EFE agency continued its unscrupulous reporting. We find in *Ya* of August 28 a rehash of the earlier story, with subtle refinements. The story was headlined "German Catholics Express Their Adherence to the Führer" and "Their Gratitude to the Troops of the Reich for Their Victorious Advance". The EFE promised, moreover, that the bishops "will publish" a pastoral letter to the faithful later in the moment of the definitive victory of the German forces. There is no mention of the fact that at this same Fulda conference the bishops had already issued a pastoral of quite a different tenor.

Decidedly, the Falangists had no need of prompting or exhortation from the bishops. But where were the bishops? The Spanish Church leaders stayed generally aloof from the "crusade" mystique. Many episcopal sees were vacant for various reasons, including assassinations during the civil war (twelve bishops were murdered). On the "crusade" there was no common reaction or collective message. The official Church organ *Ecclesia* had little to say. Its July 15 issue headed an editorial of its own "Against Atheist Russia" with the subtitle "Madrid, at the Head of All Spain, the Recruitment of Volunteers". It concluded its exhortation with "may the Lord guard the paths and the lives of our heroes." Nothing further on the subject appears in this review until November 15, when an editorial is headlined "Spanish Blood in Russia—the Blood of Spain in the Defense of Christian Civilization" and "The Historical Contribution of Catholic and Missionary Spain in the Service of Christian Civilization".

What really occupied the Spanish bishops—and the Vatican—at this time was not the war in Russia but growing signs of Nazi ideological infiltration in the country. German propaganda they found vulgar and frightening. This concern antedated the war in Russia. The papal nuncio in Madrid, Archbishop Gaetano Cicognani (brother of the apostolic delegate in Washington, Ameleto Cicognani), in reaction to an alarmed query from Cardinal Maglione of November 29, 1940, reported at great length on January 16, 1941. Important newspapers—*Arriba, Ya*—described Hitler as "the most human personage the world has ever known".

The German government, he said, had deployed great efforts to inculcate in the Spanish people the idea that the Nazi form of government was a "modern concept" and more effective. This propaganda, he continued, developed the line that although strong and victorious the Reich treated the conquered peoples with humanitarian standards. Further, it stated that it did not inhibit religion and left full liberty to Catholics even if at the same time it insisted on the observance of certain norms dictated by considerations of good order and discipline. The German propaganda in Spain, continued Cicognani, surrounded Hitler with the aureole of a great statesman—even as "a Catholic and a believer". This line of approach, reported the envoy, had made a great impression, especially on the various Falange organizations. Gifts of religious objects, mostly from the German bishops, for the restoration of churches destroyed in the civil war, ostentatiously publicized in Spain by the Reich government, also created a favorable impression.

An open apologia of the National Socialists in the Seville newspaper *Hoja del Lunes* of January 19, 1942, was the drop causing the pot to spill over. One Claudio Mariani, an author, after a trip to Germany, in the form of an "open letter to a friend in Buenos Aires" who wanted to know about the state of the Church under the Nazis, wrote, "The persecution of the Church in Germany is a wicked fable invented by enemy propaganda." The story was also carried by the Rome newspapers *Il Giornale d'Italia* and *Il Messagero* after the German embassy had asked that it be played up in the Italian Fascist press. The Vatican newspaper, *L'Osservatore Romano,* of January 22 promptly dismissed the Seville story. It said restrainedly, "Some newspapers have published information on the state of the Catholic Church in Germany. We are truly sorry to have to state that unfortunately we cannot share or confirm this evaluation." The Vatican semiofficial paper then printed in the same issue a Nazi ideological treatise, *God and Volk: A Soldier's Confession of Faith.* The nuncio in Madrid, Gaetano Cicognani got instructions to protest to the government. The nuncio also took the unusual step of circulating printed translations of the Vatican's denial and the accompanying citations from *God and Volk*. In a covering letter to the bishops, January 30, 1942, the nuncio warned of the misleading campaign in certain organs of the press on the real situation of the Church in Germany, which created the impression that there existed cordial and mutual collaboration between the two powers, the ecclesiastical and the civil, that the rights of the Church were respected, that the exercise of worship and of the sacred ministry encountered support on the part of the state, and so on. The reality, he said, is quite different. The provisions of the German concordat were not being observed. The bishops had protested, especially on the issue of the education of youth and the impediments to the pastoral ministry of the Church. Further, the nuncio regretted reports that a Spanish translation of Rosenberg's *Myth of the Twentieth Century* was in preparation—a work long since (1934) put on the Index of Forbidden Books by the Holy See.

The Vatican counteroffensive was not lost on Berlin. In his diary for April 11, 1942, Dr. Goebbels recorded:

> I have received confidential information to the effect that the Pope has appealed to the Spanish bishops under all circumstances to see to it that Spain stays out of the war. He supports his argument with humanitarian phrases. In reality he thereby gives expression to his enmity for the Axis. It is clear nonsense for a spiritual and ecclesiastical power to meddle so much in political and military questions. After the war we shall have to see to it that, as far as our country is concerned at least, such attempts at interference are rendered impossible.

Such was Goebbels' interpretation of the reactions in Rome and Madrid, on the part of the Holy See, to give the lie to German propaganda. Goebbels concluded ominously with his habitual threats of eventual reprisals "after the war".

A real annoyance for the government in Madrid was the unexpected denunciation of National Socialism itself issued by Dr. Fidel Garcia Martinez, bishop of Calahorra y La Calzada. Under date of February 28, 1942, he wrote "A Pastoral Instruction on Some Modern Errors", a vigorous criticism of the theory and practice of National Socialism. This appeared at the peak of Spain's intervention in Russia at the side of the Reich.

The Spanish press ignored the pastoral, but it got ample clandestine circulation. The Allied (especially British) and neutral press gave it worldwide publicity. In a reprint years later (October 1963) the author of the now fully vindicated instruction described his experience:

> When this instruction was first published in the church bulletin of the diocese—the first and only edition thereafter permitted—the Spanish people nearly in its entirety was the victim of a lamentable disorientation as regards the doctrines and the reality that the instruction was concerned with: the doctrines and realities that the German episcopacy, at the risk of disturbing the fatherland in the state of war, on which existence depended, were the first to denounce and condemn publicly, with truly exemplary liberty and courage, such doctrines and realities that are today a bitter memory for the noble German people.

The Spanish press, with the exception of two or three church bulletins that had the courage to reprint it, kept total silence on the instruction entitled, after the encyclical of His Holiness Pius XI of March 14, 1937, "On the Situation of the Catholic Church in the German Reich". The impression it caused on those whom it reached was truly extraordinary. Clandestine reproductions, issued without the knowledge and authorization of its author, were innumerable. Was the Spanish political leadership, Franco himself, really uninformed about the radical anti-Christian tenets of the Nazi leaders of the so-called Christian campaign? It would be more accurate to say that, like the British at this time, the new Spanish regime in its own way obeyed the political exigencies of the moment. It had to close its eyes and minimize the negative aspects of its own policy. Foreign Minister Serrano Suner appears to have recognized what Nazism was, but he found a formula to explain away to his own satisfaction the paradoxical league of Catholic Spain with the neopagan Nazi Reich. As he put it,

Nazism was a passing phenomenon and at least served to block Communism. His own closest aide, Jose Maria Doussinague, secretary general of the ministry, later recorded these confidences of his chief:

> Germany has pagan, absurd, and erroneous ideas? We know that. But this is a transient and inconsistent aberration. We ourselves have the Christian truth, which is eternal and will survive and overcome these errors. It can be the instrument that, by blocking the progress of Communism in Europe, can save this truth in Spain. In any case, we have with Germany only an alignment of circumstance, just like the English with the Russians, all of which is clearly in the sacred national interest.

Spain withdrew the last elements of its Blue Division from the *cruzada* in the spring of 1944. Apart from heavy losses and British pressure, was it also due to disillusionment?

Chapter 9

THE "FRENCH LEGION" AND
THE CASE OF CARDINAL BAUDRILLART

With military defeat in 1940, France went into a condition approaching schizophrenia. The country was divided into two zones, occupied and unoccupied. This was symbolic of a deeper split in the French soul. The traditional French passion for clear ideas got a rude challenge. A classic confrontation soon arose between those who for whatever reason accepted the legitimacy of the hero of Verdun, Marshal Philippe Pétain, as against the followers of General Charles de Gaulle, who elected to continue the war from London, hopeless as it seemed to be at the time. Worse, a dizzying reversal of alliances broke out in 1941. If Great Britain and Poland sealed an understanding with Stalin, an erstwhile ally of Hitler, the movement in France was in the opposite direction. The French Communists, who had dutifully followed the appeasing, Stalinist, pro-Hitler line since August 1939, reverted to type by abandoning their pro-German opposition to the "imperialist war" to take the road of sabotage. Vichy France moved closer to Nazi Germany. It even came to the point when right-wing extremists created an expeditionary force to fight Communism in Russia side by side with the Wehrmacht. It took the name of "Legion of French Volunteers against Bolshevism" (LVF). A famous French patriot, Cardinal Alfred Baudrillart, octogenarian rector of the Catholic Institute in Paris, warmly supported the new Legion aborning and became a leading member of its Honorary Committee of Sponsors.

On July 7, 1941, leaders of the various right-wing political parties met at the Majestic Hotel in Paris. Among them was Jacques Doriot, founder of the French Popular Party. He had been an active Communist until the mid-1930s, when he was expelled. He then went to the other end of the political rainbow. The leaders agreed to go forward with the Legion. They had an understanding with the occupation power. It was the private initiative of the parties of the occupied zone. Enthusiasm ran high, bolstered at the start by the optimistic reports from the Russian front. Recruitment went on speedily. After screening out the undesirables and the unfit (bad teeth was one of the major causes of rejection), close to three thousand of the volunteers went to a training station in Poland. The first group left Paris by train on September 4, still in their civilian clothes. On their arrival it was a revelation and a chagrin for them to be issued German uniforms. The available supply of French uniforms, it was explained to them, was "war booty" and could not be diverted.

The volunteers from then on were members of the German army. Their unit was registered in Wehrmacht rolls as the "Reinforced Infantry Regiment No. 638". This consisted of two battalions, including 181 officers and 2,271 men. Jacques Doriot was with them. A third battalion soon followed, vaguely French in composition. After a brief and necessarily superficial training they were sent to the Moscow front in the end of October. It was their misfortune to arrive at the beginning of the Red Army counteroffensive, not to speak of the offensive of "General Winter". Their losses were heavy. They were later employed in antipartisan fighting behind the lines.

This was the bloody beginning of the French Anti-Bolshevik Legion. Its end was less spectacular from the French point of view. Pétain continued to refuse support to the LVF, that is, to give it recognition or money as a French organization. In 1944 Heinrich Himmler, founder of the Waffen-SS, decided he could recognize the French as honorary Germanics. He set up a recruiting station in Paris. It had nothing to do with the LVF. The first recruits were simply misguided youths in quest of adventure. Soon it became a raid on all available French manpower. Himmler succeeded in raising his French group to the level of a division, to constitute the 33 *Waffen Grenadier Division der SS Charlemagne,* under the command of SS–Brigadeführer Gustave Kruckenberg. As for the old legionnaires of the LVF, they were incorporated into the Charlemagne without being asked. In the last days of the Nazi Reich the survivors were engaged in defensive action around Berlin. It was the end of the anti-Bolshevik mystique that promised so much in 1941.

Like Pétain, the French bishops distanced themselves from the Legion. Why should the bishops come forward when even Pétain kept his counsel? They had not been consulted. The situation was not simple. There was still the agonizing question of the thousands of prisoners of war in German hands, about whom the bishops, along with Pétain, were deeply concerned. What sense, for instance, did it make to dispatch French volunteers to Russia as German soldiers, without any reciprocity, without a finger lifted on Hitler's part toward the repatriation of these POWs?

The bishops did not even offer a chaplain to minister to the religious needs of the Legion. In this connection there emerges the flamboyant personality of Canon Jean Mayol de Lupé Caracciolo, better known simply as Mayol de Lupé, who accompanied the LVF to the Soviet front. Already retired as a military chaplain, he attached himself to the Legion without any authorization from the bishops. Press propaganda described him sometimes as a "high prelate" or even as a "bishop". He at most had an honorific title of canon of a diocese never identified. He made repeated appearances at rallies for the Legion, bemedaled, sometimes in French uniform, at other times in German uniform with a German decoration. No doubt he performed his priestly duties as chaplain with proper conscientiousness. He possibly got his legitimation as chaplain from the German military Ordinariat. In February 1945 he was in Berlin as chaplain of a Waffen-SS unit (the ex-LVF). He declared he was not prevented by the SS from exercising his priestly functions. This could have been true in a way of speaking, but it was a humiliating end to a once appealing cause. Canon Mayol de Lupé found his way back to France to face collaborationist charges.

The case of Cardinal Baudrillart is more complicated. French Catholic historians have naturally sought to explain the sudden and strange transformation of this distinguished scholar, member of the French Academy, esteemed by all. As simply rector of the Catholic Institute, even though cardinal, he had no diocesan responsibilities. But his voice as a patriot had a special meaning for the public. In 1914–18 he directed the "Catholic Committee for Propaganda Abroad". When war broke out again in 1939 he denounced Nazi atrocities in Poland with vehemence. He was not previously known for pro-German sympathies. Nor was he known for affinity with the right-wing personalities of strange background into whose company he was soon to fall.

One simple explanation is that Baudrillart was haunted by memories of the Commune of Paris in 1871, which he had seen as a boy. He often alluded to this event as a lesson for the future. It was easy for him to envisage another Commune, another civil war, in a France currently divided as it was and exposed to radical movements. It remains unclear how he was led to overlook the very real existing threat of a Nazi hegemony over all Europe as against a danger as yet much more remote. His personal drama can at least serve as symptomatic of the disorientation reigning in many minds at that time. Who knew, in fact, where France was going? With the help of notes in his own diary, it is possible to discern at least some stages of his evolution from 1940 on.

For instance, in the months immediately after the defeat he came into contact with Alphonse de Chateaubriant, editor of the new philo-German weekly of Paris, *La Gerbe*. Chateaubriant had a sort of mystic experience in the mid-1930s. It led him to esoteric interpretations of National Socialism. His new book, *La Gerbe des forces*, a plaidoyer for German-French reconciliation, caught the cardinal's attention. He was shaken, even convinced. Was it because the book answered questions and resolved doubts already in his mind?

Certainly Baudrillart was tormented by questions and doubts, as any other Frenchman in 1940. Did Chateaubriant have more clairvoyance than the rest? On September 5 the two came together with resulting closer contacts with *La Gerbe.* Another visitor came to the Catholic Institute who also, if we are to trust the diary, impressed Baudrillart. It was on November 8. The caller was a German officer, one Kurt Reichl, who presented himself as responsible for relations with the Catholic Church. He was an Austrian, not a Prussian, as Baudrillart recorded with satisfaction, with almost French manners (though he brought an interpreter with him). Suavely, Reichl assured his host that the Führer was not really anti-Catholic but that he had to defend Germany against the intrigues of the "political Church" in Germany. How Baudrillart could accept at face value this standard Nazi pretext and close his eyes to the contrary evidence is another indication of the prelate's current confusion. Reichl was a counterintelligence agent of the Nazi secret service. The occupying power a few weeks earlier had sequestered the archives of the archbishop of Paris, Cardinal Emmanuel Suhard. They had also ransacked the Catholic Institute and Baudrillart's most intimate papers. It is quite possible that both operations were done under Reichl's direction. The rifling of documents soon resulted in a Nazi propaganda book on how the French bishops themselves, like the German, had been deeply involved in politics before the war. This was a high-handed procedure—of which the two cardinals were both witness and victim—for a government protesting its desire for peace with the Church.

It was the hour of decision, as far as Baudrillart was concerned. Within a few days, on November 20, 1940, he launched an appeal to the country to support Marshal Philippe Pétain. He did it on his own impulse, without any evidence of consultation with his confreres in the episcopate. The statement, in the form of a long press release, was entitled *"Choisir. Vouloir. Obéir."* He cried out:

"Let us close ranks behind the chief and the father who today incarnates France."

It was a bombshell and naturally got maximum coverage in the Vichy press. But there are still extant letters of bitter protest, for example, from veterans of the war of 1914–18. The criticisms left him unmoved. Cardinal Suhard, who lived not so far away from him down the street, thought it better to leave his neighbor alone. But another bishop had the spirit to tell him to his face that the clergy of Paris might have great difficulty in providing for him a funeral worthy of his great services to the Church in his long and distinguished career. Cardinal Baudrillart could only shrug his shoulders and say he was simply following his conscience. He had made his choice. The same conscience was to lead him, a half-year later, to his much discussed, not to say lyric, support of the anti-Bolshevik Legion organized by Jacques Doriot and others. As the French historian Paul Christophe reviewed the situation:

> The cardinal publicly advocated cooperation with Germany. The fear of Bolshevism, the rereading of events in the light of the war of 1870 and the Commune of 1871, his concern for national unity around the marshal, the growth of his Anglophobia and of his hostility to Gaullism, his total attachment to *his* Institute, all led him to his declaration. But the influence of his readings, particularly of Alphonse de Chateaubriant, as well as the comedy perpetrated on him, banished all his last remaining doubts. With his public stand Cardinal Baudrillart had dangerously caught his finger in the gears.

The process of entrapment was inexorable. If the cardinal favored cooperation with the conqueror in 1940, Germany's sudden war against Bolshevism in 1941 could only confirm him in his decision. He soon expressed his enthusiasm with intuitions very far from the reality. In a message contributed to the first number of the new Paris weekly *Toute la Vie,* a supplement of *Le Nouveau Temps* founded by Jean Luchaire in the end of July 1941, he developed his thinking on the subject of the Anti-Bolshevik Legion:

> Priest and French, how can I, in a moment so decisive, refuse to approve the common noble enterprise directed by Germany, dedicated to liberate Russia from the bonds that have held it for the past twenty-five years, suffocating its old human and Christian traditions, to free France, Europe, and the world from the most pernicious and most sanguinary monster that mankind has ever known, to raise the peoples above their narrow interests, and to establish among them a holy fraternity revived from the time of the Christian Middle Ages?

Adolf Hitler had an entirely different conception of what he would do in a conquered Russia. His enterprise was neither common nor noble. If doubts need arise about the authenticity of the quotes attributed to Baudrillart, one can compare them with another text over which the writer had immediate control. This is found in the introduction he wrote for a member of his own Catholic Institute. Professor I.-V. Pouzyna wrote on the history of Bolshevism. The volume was issued by the "Anti-Bolshevik Action Committee". We read in a signed presentation, "The day of wrath has finally come. The civilized and Christian world rises to defend and save forever our ancient Christian society, endangered by Bolshevism, that is, in danger of perishing." The prelate continued, further, "I would be happy to participate, no matter how modestly, in the common noble enterprise designed to raise the peoples above their narrow interests and to create among them a holy fraternity, revived from the Middle Ages."

The phrase "common noble enterprise" was ideal for the propagandists on both sides, striking the imagination, for praise or for blame. Baudrillart, reaching the end of his days, was to say more surprising things. In the last months of 1941 the effort of organizing the Legion of French Volunteers against Bolshevism was going on with intensity. The cardinal's moral support was important. We find a long interview recorded by Maurice-Yvan Sicard, in *Le Cri du peuple* of December 4, 1941. This was the newspaper of Jacques Doriot. The cardinal developed at some length the history of Bolshevism, blaming England for failing to assist those who were opposed to the Bolsheviks. He also recalled the severe criticisms of atheistic Communism by Pope Pius XI. He cried out, "The Archangel Michael brandishes his avenging sword, brilliant and invincible, against the diabolical powers. With him march the old Christian and civilized peoples who defend their past and their future at the side of the German armies."

He went on:

As a priest and as a Frenchman, I dare to say that these Legionaries are among the best of the sons of France. Placed at the point of decisive combat, our Legionaries are the effective illustration of the France of the Middle Ages, of our France of the cathedrals, and I say this because I am sure these soldiers guarantee a great rebirth of France. In truth, this Legion constitutes, in its own way, a new chivalry. These Legionaries are the crusaders of the twentieth century. May their arms be blessed! The tomb of Christ will be delivered!

Such expressions obviously did not sit well with many. Indignant parish priests of Paris sent a delegation to Archbishop Cardinal Suhard to say they would not continue to send any students to the Catholic Institute if the rector continued on this line. We find a similar protest in a three-page clandestine leaflet entitled *"Veritas"*, dated August 26, 1941, and headed "Reply to Cardinal Baudrillart". It was signed "a French Catholic". The anonymous writer directed himself to the cardinal.

Eminence, in the whole Church of France you are the only one to speak. Around you the bishops, the archbishops, the cardinals are silent. Do you not perceive the reprobation by this silence over your indecent explosions? Do you not see that the press is open only to those who servilely echo German propaganda? Do you not realize that if the French episcopate does not open its mouth it is because it does not want to sing in chorus with Hitler and Goebbels?

The writer went on to observe that the crusaders of old had to confess their sins and abjure their errors before taking up the shield. Hitler had not renounced his paganism. Only a few months earlier, in his address at Easter, he said, the Pope made allusion to the "hidden persecution" that he could not catalogue because of the possibility of reprisals. Hitler, concluded the writer brutally, is a "camouflaged butcher".

Little has come down about the personal sentiments of the soldiers, the volunteers, the crusaders on the Russian front before Moscow on whom Cardinal Baudrillart based so many expectations. The high hopes were cut down cruelly by tragedy. The LVF fell upon sad days. On May 23, 1942, the cardinal died. He was buried from Notre Dame, with the presence of high Vichy officials, including Pierre Laval, and representatives of the LVF. There was no public cortege from the Catholic Institute to Notre Dame. The body was transferred by night. It was returned also by night to the Institute for burial. The mystique of the "Anti-Bolshevik Legion" was buried with him.

Before leaving the subject of the "common noble enterprise", it is relevant to record that it pleased some writers in later years to attribute this kind of language, quite mistakenly, to Pope Pius XII. For instance, John Toland wrote in his book *Adolf Hitler,* "The Pope's attitude was not at all vague. He made it clear that he backed the Nazi fight against Bolshevism, describing it as high-minded gallantry in defense of the foundations of Christian culture." This was an egregious slip on the author's part. The wartime Pope never said anything of the kind. Pius XII knew the real direction of Hitler's war in the East, even if Baudrillart did not.

Chapter 10

FATIMA IN 1942–1944:
"RUSSIA WILL BE CONVERTED"

A single word, *icon,* used by Pope Pius XII in a discourse in 1942 set in motion a wave of rumors, speculation, and propaganda all over Europe to the end of the war. The case illustrates how, in time of war, prophecies or pseudoprophecies can create a train of unforeseen and uncontrollable practical effects. This was the destiny of Fatima, the remote Portuguese village where the Virgin Mary was said to have appeared to three peasant children. She foretold certain future developments and concluded that "Russia will be converted and there will be peace." The vision actually occurred in 1917, but a part of the message—that referring to Russia—became known to the public only in 1942. Why 1942?

It is said that the custodians of the message acted quite spontaneously, although the progress of the war could have had something to do with the decision, even in neutral Portugal. Those who were privileged to publish the text first were aware of the possible explosive political consequences. Accordingly they took the unorthodox liberty of suppressing the very word *Russia* in their first editions. In any event Pius XII had nothing to do with the disclosure, as far as is known. But a solemn commemoration of the apparition gave him the appropriate occasion, for the first time, to allude to Russia, ever so indirectly. Did he expect the explosion that was to follow?

There could be no mistaking that the Pope referred to Russia.

The icon is the characteristic sacred image in Russian religious culture. But it was the first time since the war began that the Pontiff allowed himself to make more than generic allusions to things Russian. In the first months of the war, in 1939, to the great wrath of the Poles and the French, he did not mention the Russian invader that had just carved up Poland in agreement with Nazi Germany. In 1941 he likewise avoided the word. It was not until a radio message to Portugal of October 31, 1942, that he broke his self-imposed reserve. Addressing the Virgin the Pope prayed:

> To the people separated in error or discord, and especially to those who profess the most singular devotion to you, and among whom there was not a house where thy venerable icon was not seen (today perhaps hidden and kept for better days), give them peace and bring them again to the one fold of Christ, under the one true Shepherd.

Though in appearance only slipped in parenthetically at the last moment, as if of casual significance, and that in connection with the centuries-old schism dividing the Eastern and Western Churches, the word *icon* worked like a firebrand. The press, the diplomats, the secret intelligence, the governments, and the belligerent of all sides saw political significance. Believers of course read it as a prophecy of the future state of Communism. Did this foresee the eventual crushing of the Soviet Union by the Nazis, or, on the contrary, did it foresee the conversion of Russia through the eventual victory of the United Nations?

At a time of difficult communications across hostile lines, it is surprising how quickly the Fatima message and the Pope's nod to Russia reached the farthest ends of Europe. Popular imagination did the rest. In Italy two books on the "message" came out in repeated printings. The theme of the conversion of Russia was particularly appealing in Italy. It could signify the eventual success of the Italian forces in Russia and, with it, peace. In Germany, however, Nazi observers had a less positive reaction about the Fatima message or the Pope's allusion to an icon. The Gestapo, always suspicious of every papal move, perceived a threat in the Pope's passing mention of the icon and the consecration to the Immaculate Heart of Mary that ensued. In the mobilization of prayer, they saw a danger—first for Italy and then also for the German home front. They watched with growing misgivings as the consecrations multiplied throughout Italy and then, soon, also in France, now completely occupied by the Nazis. The same occurred in Belgium and in Holland, and even in the Reich—with increasingly anti-Nazi and "defeatist" implications.

One could possibly suppose that the sentiments of pious Catholics devoted to the Virgin Mary, originating in the Portuguese hinterlands and saluted religiously by the Pope, with an aside on icons, created no fears for the Gestapo. It was not so. In normal moments, perhaps. But these were critical weeks. The winds of war, hitherto in favor of the Axis, were blowing in the opposite direction. Early, on December 18, 1942, the chief of the Gestapo, Heinrich Müller, alerted the Foreign Ministry. His report bore the title "Circulation of a Peace Prayer by Pius XII in Italy". The Pope's talk on October 31, he said, could be linked to the Anglo-American offensive in North Africa. Catholic Action in Italy, he went on, was vigorously promoting the prayer, with the help of "an indulgence of three years and a plenary indulgence to be gained once a month for those reciting it". This was entirely too sinister for the Gestapo, which thought Wilhelmstrasse should know about it. This action, Müller alleged, was aided and abetted by the enemy. The prayer, alleged Müller further, corresponded to "all the pacifist and cosmopolitan initiatives" of the Italian bishops and other clergy, with the effect of undermining the people's will to resist. Heinrich ("Gestapo") Müller wrote:

The prayer is directed on the one hand against "the invading of neopaganism, which is all materialist", that is, in Church terminology, against National Socialism. And on the other hand, it exhibits what is, for the Italian people at this moment in the current morale situation, a highly objectionable and dangerous pacifist appeal to peace at any price.

Thus, from the beginning, the consecration to the Immaculate Heart of Mary, with the theme of the "conversion of Russia" in the background, took on a predominantly pacifist, Resistance, anti-Axis, philo-Allied, and also philo-Soviet connotation. The record to this effect in the coming weeks is eloquent. In Belgium, Cardinal Joseph van Roey, archbishop of Malines, in a pastoral of February 20, 1943, urged the consecration, citing the papal address and the indulgenced prayer, with its mention of the icon. The German propagandists attempted to transform this call into support for the "anti-Bolshevik crusade". So flagrant was the misrepresentation, particularly in propaganda directed to Holland, that van Roey on February 27 had to denounce these methods with a denial in the official archdiocesan bulletin. The Dutch bishops in a pastoral of May 12, 1943, protesting the deportation of workers to Germany, used the Pope's Fatima talk as a way of rejecting Nazi calls for a crusade against the "Bolshevik threat". The only crusade the bishops recognized, they said, was the crusade of prayers to the Immaculate Heart of Mary.

In England the Pope's words were explained and generously interpreted in the form to be expected. Cardinal Arthur Hinsley of Westminster (London) was one of the first. This is how the English prelate (and the BBC in broadcasts to Germany) expounded the Pope's invitation to prayer:

> The Holy Father alludes unmistakably to Russia, whose people are now heroically defending their hearth and homes against the invaders. For Russia we plead daily in our prayers after Mass. Let us redouble our prayers now that the age-old devotion of the Russian people to the Mother of God—alive still, even though dormant—in so many of their hearts, may earn for them her especial protection in these days and restore them soon to union with her Divine Son.

One can understand that in Berlin these words were presented as if the Catholic prelate were praying for Russia. Hinsley was referring to the three "Hail Marys" that the late Pontiff Pius XI had ordered to be said at the end of Mass, in the 1930s, at the time of the fierce persecutions in Russia. It is hard to say if the Goebbels agency was aware of this prayer, which predated the war. It would have made no difference. Berlin even found a way to allege that the English cardinal's words were a gesture of solidarity with the Red Army, which on February 23 celebrated its twenty-fifth anniversary.

The psychological and political situation in France was very particular. All France was now occupied by the German forces. Public confusion was greater than ever. And at this time there came into circulation rumors of a vision of the Virgin that had something—just what or how was not clear to everyone—to do with the war in Russia. Was this the end, the beginning of the end? Collaborationist forces endeavored to give this vague information on Fatima an anti-Soviet ring. The Resistance, now emboldened, worked in the opposite direction. A revealing witness of the moods of the times is discerned in an editorial in the pro-Vichy *L'Action Française*. In its issue of February 18, 1944, editorialist L. Delébecque commented on a letter received from a woman reader:

> Apropos of a letter of the Sovereign Pontiff, read, it appears, and commented on in many churches, in which the Pope spoke of Fatima, that young Portuguese girl [*sic*] to whom the Holy Virgin has appeared and about revelations that the seer is said to have made to Pius XII, there is a lot of fantasy that unfortunately is not at all harmless. "I hear around me and also from afar", writes a woman correspondent, "that the successes of the Russians are due to the Holy Virgin, that there is nothing to fear from the Russians, that they will invade Europe like Catholic crusaders to reestablish order and religion." Communist Russia will be converted, and, thanks to Russia, after the war there will be a spiritual renewal in the Church. That being so, the Communist danger "does not exist".

The Vichy editorialist gave vent to his exacerbation at such naïveté: "We cannot afford just to shrug our shoulders. I repeat, such utterances, spread around and elaborated, can shake insecure minds; they can cause damage in the moral order, which will bring along with it new disasters in the material order."

One can sympathize with the writer, whose alarm was all too justified. The French public was highly vulnerable to such currents, and the government was powerless to stop the rumors. The disturbance was felt not only in popular circles. We gather from a keen contemporary observer an understanding of what the Fatima message meant for many French intellectuals. It appears to have had a charm that had transfixed them.

Writing in the Paris monthly *Études* of February 1945, that is, after the liberation of Paris and before the end of the war, the Jesuit Gaston Fessard gave an illuminating account of the drama with which we are dealing, as it concerned Catholic French intellectuals. Fatima, in brief, reached into the heart of the Catholic cultural milieu at a crucial moment. He described how and why the simple short prayer of consecration, with its mention of the icon, had profound significance for so many:

> The occupation authorities did not discover until belatedly the poison of these two short paragraphs. Sharp as were the minds of the Gestapo, how could they imagine that such an anathema could slip into a prayer as innocent as a consecration to the Virgin Mary? In February 1943, sensing the immense weight of the text that the Pope offered to the universal Church as the theme of her perpetual prayer, they tried to prohibit not its publication (already issued three months earlier) but its further diffusion in tracts and by public lectures. In vain. In all the churches of France, on March 25, the Feast of the Annunciation, or on the following Sunday, the consecration to the Immaculate Heart of Mary was officially read. German propaganda was reduced to spreading false rumors in order to play down the importance of this text or to display its ill humor in trying to change its nature. It succeeded only in bringing out all the more the value of this prayer in which the French conscience found unchallengeable confirmation of the attitude that its love of the common good had instinctively suggested to them.

For Fessard, the papal words were sympathetic to the Soviets and hostile to the Nazis. They released him, and many French, from a perplexity that had beset them since Hitler's attack on the Soviet Union in 1941. Those words were expressly critical of "neopaganism", whereas the Pope was silent on Soviet "atheistic materialism", speaking unexpectedly instead of the "icon". For intellectuals living in occupied France, Fessard considered, the moral situation was at last clear, thanks to the few short words of the papal consecration: "In the conflict between Germany and Russia, who could wish for a clearer condemnation of Hitler as an unjust aggressor or a more unmistakable denunciation of the role played by Nazism in the series of injustices that bloodied the soil of Europe?"

The issue exploded again in May as the consecrations, organized by the bishops, continued. The Axis press denied rumors spread by Anglo-American agencies that the Pope himself had ordered prayers for Russia. The *Semaine Catholique* of Fribourg, Switzerland, scoffed at the allegations. It recalled that since 1930 the then Pope, Pius XI, had designated prayers at the end of Mass "for Russia". If there were any prayers for Russia, it was for Russia's conversion.

In Germany, Catholics could hardly be expected to pray openly for the victory of the Red Army, but their own devotion to Mary was a legitimate outlet for their sentiments. There, too, the consecrations went forward. The Gestapo continued to be outraged. It was reduced to trivial complaints that railroad traffic was overburdened by the number of alleged religious pilgrims. On May 12, Himmler's Reich Main Security Office sent another warning to the Foreign Ministry, bringing the Fatima affair up to date. This was a twenty-page ideological harangue, ending with a ritualistic denunciation also of Jews, plutocrats, Bolsheviks, and other enemies of the state:

> The whole Fatima propaganda is directed in its structure against the fundamental principles of National Socialism. This deserves special attention because according to a *Kipa* [Swiss Catholic news agency] dispatch of May of this year, the propagandistic exploitation of the "Fatima visions" is to begin in Germany, with a consecration of the German dioceses. This propaganda

is therefore especially dangerous because through this the democratic war criminals, who started the war, are exculpated and the war effort through arms is presented as worthless and superfluous.

Yet a third intelligence report on this subject can be cited to establish the widespread impact of the Pope's consecration prayer of the Fatima secret. This is signed by Ernst Kaltenbrunner, Heydrich's successor as head of the entire Nazi police and party intelligence organization, the Reich Main Security Office (RSHA). It is dated earlier, on April 21, 1943, and was prepared by the Vatican desk of the Nazi intelligence. From Zagreb (Croatia), said the report, came the news that the Vatican had given instructions to the Croatians to cease anti-Bolshevik propaganda and to stop opposing Russia. The Pope thought, according to the informant, "that Russia will find its way back to God as a result of the hard trials of this war". As for Fatima, the informant said that at the same time the Catholic Church will cause the prophecies of Fatima (known to the Foreign Ministry as "the miracle of Fatima") to be printed and distributed. In these prophecies can be found places at which it is said the Russians will be converted and will be healed "by the wounded heart of the Mother of God".

Even in 1944 the consecration continued to vex and even haunt the Nazi chiefs. After the attempt on Hitler's life on July 20, the Fatima syndrome returned. We find in a Gestapo report of August 10 this revealing speculation:

> The suspicions arose in party circles, immediately after the *Attentat* on the Führer, that certain leads link these prophecies to the perpetrators. . . . In any case, the legend of the visions of Fatima, only now after twenty-seven years made known to wide circles and in connection with the rumor of the great transition of the war, was quite widely circulated on July 13.

The Pope's one word, *icon,* clearly was a floating mine, touching off unpredictable explosions in a wide variety of situations in both camps.

Chapter 11

COMMUNISM'S NEW FACE IN 1943

Propaganda begets counterpropaganda. This was seen in an earlier chapter when the "crusade" of June 1941 was matched on the Allied side by mobilization of Christianity against Nazism. In 1943, as the Nazis sought throughout Europe to sow fear of a Bolshevik mastery of the Continent, the Soviet regime itself made at least two significant and sensational gestures or concessions to world opinion, reaping immediate results. On May 23, 1943, *Pravda* announced the disbanding or suppression of the Third Communist International, the much-feared Comintern, Moscow's notorious instrument for fomenting world revolution. And a few months later, on September 5, *Izvestia* published a notice that on the previous day Metropolitan Sergei of Moscow, in company with the archbishops of Leningrad and Kiev, had been received by Stalin. Permission, said the paper, had been granted for the convoking of a council of bishops for the purpose of electing a Patriarch of Moscow. This prestigious office of the "Third Rome" had been vacant since the death of Tykhon in the mid-1920s because of lack of Stalin's approval. The election of Sergei himself ensued with notable speed on September 8, followed by an equally expeditious enthronement on September 12.

These two events struck world imagination profoundly. Was the leopard changing its spots? Sceptics there were in great number, but optimists in equal number. Had Stalin really given up the Marxist program for world revolution? Had this archpersecutor now repented of his war against the Church and all religious belief? Or was it all a masquerade, a tactical move?

The Comintern had indeed been sorely tried by the Molotov-Ribbentrop pact of August 1939 and was reduced to enforced inaction, both during the Nazi-Soviet honeymoon of 1939–41 and equally so after the Anglo-Soviet alliance of July 1941. It had a bad name even among the national parties, and its end was dictated almost as much by party considerations as by the requirements of world politics. The British and Americans, as was to be expected, welcomed the news as a sign of Stalin's readiness to turn a new page in history. They saw in this the triumph of Russian nationalism as against world revolution that had held primacy for so long. If nothing more, some of the more sceptical observers thought, the winding up of the Comintern might prove irreversible, even if initially evoked for purely tactical reasons. It was noted, however, that shortly afterward *Pravda* wrote the assurances that the national parties (not, of course, dissolved) were fully able to continue their leadership of the working class, the proletariat, independently. It was to be seen in the postwar years that Stalin did not really intend to loosen his hold on the world Communist movement. Even after the Comintern's demise he kept tight control on the parties abroad with imperious directives that brooked no questioning, giving a stark connotation to the word *Stalinism*.

The restoration of the Moscow Patriarch responded to a profound evolution of the Russian peoples, of which Stalin himself was not entirely master and arbiter. The hardships and sufferings of the war had awakened a great religious thirst that could not be ignored by the party chiefs, least of all as the Germans seemed victorious on all fronts. The majority of Russian believers rallied to what they saw as the national and patriotic cause of Holy Russia. By mid-1943 the Kremlin's attitude toward the Orthodox, once stigmatized in Soviet anti-church propaganda as the fifth column of Czarism, had softened. The possibility, or better, the necessity, loomed that the Orthodox Church of Russia could serve for the regime the same role it had served in Czarist times among the fraternal Orthodox communities of the Soviet Union's neighbors. Already in 1942 Sergei had proved himself useful in contacts not only with the Church of England but with the various other Orthodox jurisdictions such as the Patriarchates of Constantinople, Jerusalem, Alexandria, and Antioch. On Easter 1942 he had addressed himself to the Rumanian Orthodox, exhorting them to throw off the alliance with Germany. Similar calls went to the Christians of Yugoslavia, Czechoslovakia, Greece, and other countries in the German sphere. Appeals to resist were broadcast by Moscow radio. In the same summer of 1943, Sergei, still only metropolitan, appeared with six other bishops at the All-Slav congress in Moscow. In these circumstances, the restoration of the Patriarchate indicated Stalin was finding the religious prestige of the Church very helpful, especially in the foreign field. One of the first acts (September 19) of the new Patriarch was to receive a delegation from the Church of England, headed by the archbishop of York, Cyril Foster Garbett.

On these developments, the *Journal de Genève* (September 13) offered this intuition to its readers:

> In adopting a more liberal attitude toward the Church, the Soviet leaders have at the same time a national and an international aim in view: to strengthen the national front and to improve their position in the Balkan countries. They make very clever use of Panslavism by reminding the occupied Slav countries that Russia is their mother. Thus the Kremlin prepares the way for an increase of its influence in that area by making use of the Eastern Church for which, since the fall of Constantinople, Moscow represents the Holy City. . . . Through this masterly move, which means the renewal of the ancient alliance between Orthodoxy and imperial politics, Stalin may have frustrated all attempts to create the *cordon sanitaire,* which haunts and irritates him.

All this, of course, must be read in the war context. The Council, or Synod of Bishops, which elected Sergei also decreed the unfrocking of bishops and of priests who had collaborated with the Germans and the excommunication of laity guilty of the same crime. In addition, they made an appeal that was carried by the Soviet press and Moscow radio. They declared: "Assembled in Moscow to appoint a Patriarch of the Russian Orthodox Church, the Synod sends out a call to the Christians of the whole world: 'Let us unite in the name of Christianity for victory. . . . The Orthodox Church asks the collaboration of all Christians in the destruction of Hitlerism.' "

Only nineteen bishops actually took part in the Synod, partly no doubt because of the haste in which it was convoked and the difficulties of travel but also because the number of bishops still at liberty after years of persecution was limited. Some bishops were consecrated on short notice. For all this, the reaction abroad was as significant in the Reich as it was in London and Washington, if in a different sense. Martin Bormann, head of the Nazi party chancellery in Berlin, saw the election as a Bolshevik maneuver, evident also in other ways, to use religion for political purposes. In a circular of October 20, entitled "Religion as a Cover for Politics", he warned of the new tactic and pointed out its political aspect, for example, the condemnation of Nazi collaborators. He also noted the use of religious themes by clandestine radio stations, such as the Free German Committee, the Polish-language Christian Radio, the Spanish radio that called itself Catholic Action under the Protection of Our Lady of the Pillar, and similar broadcasts by Hungarian and Bulgarian stations.

Stalin's revival of the top religious office in the land was piously considered a tribute extorted from the Soviet dictator. The Russian Orthodox archbishop in Berlin itself, Seraphim, declared reasonably enough, "The fact that Stalin is now seeking a pact with the Church proves . . . that the Bolsheviks have not succeeded in annihilating the spirit of Orthodoxy." The ferociously anti-Soviet journal for "Russian Orthodox outside of Russia", *Pravoslavnaya Rus,* published in Slovakia, affirmed that the concession showed the Soviets had to yield to the spirit of the people who, after years of patriotic struggle, were now trying also to give effect to their religious aspirations. The change in church policy, it declared, was proof that the Church in Russia "had won a tremendous victory—comparable to that in the age of Constantinople when the martyrs of the Church broke the evil will of their imperial persecutors".

It recalled, however, that the new Patriarch Sergei was himself personally suspect because of his long record of subservience to the government. This charge, it hastened to add, could not be made against his colleagues in the Church of Russia. The emigré organ in Slovakia said it awaited word from the Patriarch concerning the martyrs of the recent past and about the liberation of those imprisoned for the Faith.

In this flurry of surprise and poorly disguised satisfaction in Orthodox circles, even in the German sphere of influence, the campaign of Goebbels, portraying in somber colors the fate of a Bolshevik-dominated Europe, lost some of its effectiveness. Indeed, if Stalin was willing to make peace with the Orthodox of his own country, why could he not also consider reconciliation with the Catholic Church? Rumors of the kind began to be ventilated even before, at the time of the dissolution of the Comintern.

The archbishop of New York, Francis Spellman (on a tour of the Middle East to visit U.S. Catholic troops), was actually reported to have seen Smirnov, the Soviet ambassador at Teheran. German sources had their own version of the Spellman trip. On May 4, Consul General Twardowski reported from Istanbul that the New York prelate had declared himself concerned over the growing influence of Bolshevism in the area. Twardowski claimed that Spellman finally got the Vatican's consent for his trip "to study the threat to the Catholic Church through Bolshevism". The archbishop was reported to have received a pessimistic impression. The *Basler Nachrichten* of May 6 claimed to know that the purpose of Spellman's tour was to persuade the Pope that the Soviets and their armies were not so bad as the Vatican thought. "If this was the purpose," wrote the correspondent, honestly enough, "he would have done better to stay in New York."

The Washington correspondent of the *Times* (London) wrote to his newspaper on May 25, 1943, "There is also a persistent report that a concordat between Russia and the Vatican is in the making. Those who believed the story pointed out that Archbishop Spellman was then in Turkey, at no great distance from Moscow, and insisted, rightly or wrongly, that some form of agreement with the Soviets would be welcome to the Church." As we know now, no concordat was "in the making", and the story is an interesting instance of how news can be guided to suit official policy.

Two days later, the *New York Times* carried a story by its own man in Washington, Harold Callender, who topped the speculation with these words:

> Some of those in closest touch with Russian relations believe that the dissolution of the Communist International may be followed by some gesture in the religious field calculated to allay suspicion of Moscow abroad. This might take the form, they say, of an understanding with the Vatican, possibly a concordat, permitting freedom for Catholic schools and monastic orders in Russia.

If the Callender dispatch had any basis, it would have been the U.S. State Department and was really directed at Moscow as a hint on how to deal with the religious question.

This was a time of general perplexity about Stalin's intentions. Churchill reflected this, with his famous remark about the inscrutability of the Russian mind. A contemporary newspaper cartoon accurately described the situation with a sketch of the Soviet dictator in front of a mass of newspaper clippings and sighing, "It is getting more and more difficult to remain an enigma."

To this incomplete catalogue of highly speculative, contradictory, and tendentious news stories of what deserves to be called a "silly season", we can add a last odd sample. On April 2, a Geneva newspaper ascribed to British sources a report that a delegation of no fewer than seven Soviet representatives had arrived at the Vatican. The reader is expected to understand that they had come on the Vatican's invitation to negotiate. It was not explained how they could have arrived at their destination, passing through enemy lines. But a useful purpose was served by this cryptic report in the propaganda war of the time.

Chapter 12

A PERSISTENT LIE:
THE "SECRET PACT" OF 1941

From the start, in mid-1941, Hitler swore he would not let a single Catholic priest enter the Soviet Union he was so sure of overrunning. No amount of propaganda advantage about a "crusade" could compensate for the prospect of Vatican emissaries profiting from the military situation in order to evangelize Russia. The very idea was abhorrent. The evidence of the Führer's mind on this subject is multiple—in the words and orders of Hitler, in the reports of the security police, in the statements of local Nazi commissars, in the archives of the Foreign Ministry and of the German embassy to the Holy See. All this notwithstanding, there arose the astounding affirmation, during the war and afterward, that the Nazi Reich and the Holy See had entered into an agreement of mutual assistance in Russia. The Führer was said to have offered the Vatican every facility in return for the moral support of the Pope in his "crusade". How an egregious falsehood of this kind could persist long after the record was known is a sad commentary on the prevailing ignorance of the mind of Hitler—as also of the mind of Pius XII—and, in general, of the general lack of grasp at that time of the fanatical hostility of the Nazis against the Catholic Church. The survival of the legend or the lie also suggests the extent of willful ideological prejudice, above all in intellectual circles elsewhere, when the Catholic Church is concerned.

The literary history of this legend takes its start already in 1941

and grows thereafter. It was a legend that fed on itself, with
various writers borrowing from each other, and always without
any documentary proof. There was a certain plausibility to the
story line in the context of current propaganda. Were not Nazism
and the Vatican at one in their opposition to Bolshevism? What
could seem more natural and intelligent than for the two parties
to enter into an understanding at this moment? Plausible or not,
it was completely foreign to the ideology of Hitler.

Strange as it may seem, the stage for the hoax of an alleged
agreement on the sending of priests to Russia with Hitler's approval
was set thanks to a Rome dispatch of an American news agency,
the United Press. In a story datelined "Vatican City", July 29, it
reported as follows:

> A delegation of Catholic priests, specially trained to do mis-
> sionary work in Russian territory occupied by the German
> armies and their allies, have arrived in Hungary and Rumania
> en route to their new posts, high Vatican sources reported here
> today. The priests who have been studying at the Russian
> College in Rome will enter occupied territory as soon as
> military authorities grant permission, it was said. Other priests
> in Rome are ready to join them.

The same UP dispatch was also carried outside the United
States, for example, in the Swiss *Neue Zürcher Zeitung*. United
Press in Rome at that time was represented by Reynolds and
Eleanor Packard. In their book published on their return to
America after Pearl Harbor under the title *Balcony Empire,* they
amplified their original report in these terms:

> We learned while still in Rome that a number of priests had
> already gone into those parts of Russia that had been occupied
> by the German army, and were endeavoring to spread the
> Catholic religion. One Vatican authority told us that the Holy
> See did not regard this as taking a political stand, but simply as
> part of its fundamental policy of sending Catholic missionaries
> wherever they were permitted to go, regardless of the circum-
> stances. The Germans were willing to allow priests to carry

out their missionary work because they believed there were many Russians and Ukrainians who secretly yearned for religion, and that therefore if the German army was followed by priests, it would help reconcile the Russians to German occupation.

The same recital, signed by only Eleanor Packard, was published in the January 1943 issue of a monthly, *American Magazine.* Both versions were destined to be amply elaborated on by Soviet propagandists. Up to this point, a formal "agreement" was not asserted. This was, however, a logical sequel, and it came from Vichy. Paul Gentizon, a well-known journalist, in his column "Lettre d'Italie" for *Le Temps* (Lyons) of October 8, wrote on this subject under the heading "The Holy See and Bolshevism". According to him:

> As concerns the Baltic front, negotiations between the Holy See and the German occupation authorities have had a favorable outcome. Already the first priests have left Rome and have reached their destination. In Catholic circles around the Vatican there is satisfaction about this development, which allows the Holy See to have new direct contacts with millions of faithful. In the regions that reach from the Baltic to the Black Sea, the Church finds herself before an immense task. A new field of action is opening up to the Holy See as well as to all the virtues of Christian charity.

This was several months after the opening of the war—time enough for doubts to arise. That Gentizon could write so confidently at such a late date can be attributed to the political turmoil of the times as well as to the confusion in men's minds as to what Hitler intended to do in Russia. In nonoccupied (Vichy) France, there was also a definite interest in fancying such a development, which could justify the collaborationism of the Pétain regime.

The alleged "Catholic circles around the Vatican" could not have been responsible officials, or they would have known better. This was a time of complete stalemate in Berlin-Vatican relations. There were no negotiations of any kind with "a favorable outcome", let alone a deal for missionary work supported by

Hitler. Requests for authorization for Catholic priests ran up against a stone wall. Those few apostolic men who slipped across the border illegally and clandestinely into Russia from Poland, Estonia, or Slovakia were arrested as soon as they were discovered and deported back to from where they came; others were not heard of again and presumed killed. Soon Hitler, with a military order of August 6 signed by Field Marshal Wilhelm Keitel of the High Command, strictly limited the contacts of the Wehrmacht with the civilian populations in the religious sphere. More importantly as a sign of Hitler's mind, it was further forbidden to the army to allow, or invite to the occupied zones, civilian priests either from the Reich or from elsewhere.

The August 6 order was occasioned by the army's unauthorized public reopening of several churches in a few cities of White Russia and Ukraine in the first days of the offensive. The *Führerbefehl* makes hash of the alleged Vatican agreement. (The relative military and police orders aiming to block religious work by Catholics in occupied Russia are amplified in the next chapter.)

Even after the war, the Gentizon piece was taken at face value and utilized in a book, *Messages de Guerre,* by Gabriel Louis Jaray. This was a collection of various papal wartime discourses. In an introductory essay, the editor wrote, "After the German army occupied parts of Russia, the Vatican concluded with Berlin an agreement authorizing the Catholic missionaries of the Russicum [the Russian College in Rome] to go to the occupied territories and putting the Baltic territories in the sphere of competence of the nunciature of Berlin." The presumed author of the essay had been president of the Comité France-Amérique. Curiously, he wrote in quite a different sense during the war, in his committee's monthly bulletin, *American Nations:* "It is said that Germany offered to the Vatican the monopoly of this evangelization in the Russian-occupied regions. It seems that this is not the case. The presence of a prince of the Bulgarian Church in Germany is believed to be in relation to the efforts, said to be crowned with success, of the Bulgarian Orthodox Church to assume in charge there the re-Christianization of occupied Russia." For his source the editor referred to the Swiss *Basler Nachrichten* of March 27, 1942. The "monopoly" is therefore alleged to be handed over by Hitler not to the Vatican but to the Bulgarians—an offer as imaginary as the earlier Vatican "pact".

The rumor mill continued to grind. A dispatch of October 8, 1941, was sent by the Polish news agency PAT from Stockholm to the *Dziennik Polski,* the London newspaper of the free Poles. It cited information received by the *Svenska Dagbladet* from its Berlin correspondent to the effect that the Germans were willing to offer the Vatican the privilege of sending its missionaries into Russia as the price of support for their cause. This unfactual story from Dr. Goebbels' kitchen ricocheting across wartime Europe was taken seriously in the October official organ "Polish Feature and News Service" in an article concerning concessions to the Poles in Russia—that is, about chaplains for Polish troops in Russia negotiated by the London Poles with Stalin at this time. It stated, "Hitler has been quick to seize on this latter point, and he is trying to get into the good graces of the Vatican by offering to allow Roman Catholic missionaries free entrance into the German-occupied territories of Russia. This would be a realization of one of the Vatican's most cherished desires." Such ready credibility on news from "Sweden" suggests how great was the cloud of unknowing in these months.

In this exhibit of unfounded and false newspaper reports, a special classification belongs to the brainstorming of an imaginative and unscrupulous Roman journalist by the name of Virgilio Scattolini. This tipster made fools of a host of foreign correspondents, diplomats, and secret agents in the Italian capital from 1939 to 1948. In the span of ten years he sold to gullible clients descriptions of Vatican doings and correspondence—in reality all fabricated by himself. His red-faced victims one after the other nursed their wounds and kept silent, while he sought and always found new outlets. His definitive exposure came only after the war, when the Italian Communists published on their own initiative large anti-Vatican selections of his confidential bulletins, which he called *Notiziari*. These appeared during the crucial electoral campaign in the spring of 1948 in two volumes entitled *The Secret Diplomacy of the Vatican*. A torrent of astonished and indignant denials poured out from persons named. Identified at last as the author, Scattolini was sentenced to six months in jail, and his remarkable career was over. But his innumerable *Notiziari* remain in diplomatic and intelligence archives today, not to speak of newspaper files, constituting a veritable minefield for unwary researchers. Eager book buyers for American libraries gobbled up copies of the limited edition of the two volumes, and they can be found, for instance, in the U.S. Library of Congress and the New York Public Library.

Scattolini's greatest conquest was to be enlisted by the U.S. Office of Strategic Services (OSS) in 1944 to supply them with dispatches reaching the Vatican from Tokyo, which he assured them he could provide through mysterious contacts. It was easy for him to oblige his employers, since the bulletins came out of his own fertile imagination—a colossal swindle that went on for months at the expense of the Americans. The Rome base of the OSS was headed by James Jesus Angleton, later CIA counterintelligence chief. He budgeted five hundred dollars monthly for this illusory service. OSS Chief General William Donovan was so delighted with Angleton's *coup* that he took care to send copies to the White House, as can be seen in OSS papers released to the public years later.

Other specimens of the *Notiziari* are found in the archives of the German Foreign Ministry. Some of them are marked "submitted to the Führer [*hat dem Führer vorgelegen*]". The German ambassador to the Holy See, Diego von Bergen, received his own texts, to which, for a time, he accorded full confidence. In one of them, dated September 11, 1941, Scattolini asserted confidently that a special consultation had taken place in the Vatican on the points where Vatican policy was said to differ from that of the British. Point four had the heading "The Beginning of Negotiations with Germany for the Reestablishment of Religious Worship in the Regions of Russia Occupied by the German Invasion". According to the informant, "The negotiations signify an implicit recognition of the changes that have taken place, by military action, in Russia—changes that England of course does not recognize, since she has engaged herself in the alliance with Moscow not to conclude peace until all the territories that belong to Russia are recovered from Germany and its allies."

At this stage, von Bergen was in the dark as to any such "negotiations" or "recognition". In a telegram of September 17, that is, a week after the above notice, he inquired in perplexity about this matter. The Wilhelmstrasse was equally surprised. It replied categorically that "nothing is known" of any negotiations about the "entry of priests from Rome to the occupied territories".

But Scattolini had hit on a promising theme. A further bulletin of October 10, properly self-described as "exclusive", developed the line. "Agreements have been reached", it confided without qualification,

> between the pontifical commission for Russia, located in Vatican City, and the government of the Reich, through the apostolic nunciature in Berlin, looking forward to the reestablishment of the Church hierarchy in some parts of Russia occupied by the Germans. The various apostolic administrators, who had replaced the regularly constituted bishops of Czarist times, would be restored to their posts from which they had been expelled in the 1930s by the Soviets.

The writer then solemnly enumerated the said expelled administrators, whose names he needed only to copy from the current *Annuario Pontificio*. He concluded his fanciful sortie with the assurance that "as soon as possible the respective bishops and archbishops would be nominated in agreement with the German authorities". In normal times, such a story, allegedly derived from confidential Vatican sources, would have been immediately dismissed as unworthy of belief. But with the formidable Wehrmacht advancing rapidly toward Moscow, the information could impress a generation hungry for news.

A late contribution to the legend of the "pact" with Hitler was made by a correspondent in London. We come to know of this through a report of the apostolic delegate in the British capital, Archbishop (later Cardinal) William Godfrey. In early January 1942, the delegate wrote to the Vatican asking for verification of certain information he had received. A German refugee journalist living in London had prepared an article on this subject. He was J. C. Maier-Hultchin (J. K. Hulczynski). Before the war he had been editor of a German-language weekly in Katowice, Poland, called *Der Deutsche in Polen.* Maier-Hultchin asserted in his up-to-then unpublished manuscript, "The Reich Chancellor Hitler, before the war against Russia, to pose as the defender of Christianity against Bolshevism, had asked the Vatican to name a bishop for the territories occupied by his troops and that the Holy See had accepted the invitation by naming Canon Mark Glaser, a Rumanian canon." Godfrey said he had read the article closely and noted that the author cited no authority for his assertion. He warned the Vatican, however, that publication would be harmful for the Holy See by creating the impression that the Church had associated herself with the "Hitlerian crusade against Bolshevism".

The only specific instance that the German exile, who worked for British radio (BBC), cited was that of Glaser, and it concerned not the Soviet Union but Transnistria, seized by the Soviets from Rumania in 1940 and now recovered. The Vatican secretary of state, Cardinal Maglione, flatly denied the alleged situation. Replying on March 14, 1942, the top Vatican official was curt and clear: "No agreement has been made between the Holy See and the German Reichschancellor, either before or after the beginning of the Russo-German hostilities, on the matter of spiritual assistance to the faithful of the territories evacuated by the Soviet troops." He explained that Mark Glaser, rector of the seminary of Jasy (Rumania), had been sent on a temporary mission and it was to territory in Rumanian, not German, control. Monsignor Glaser, he continued, went to his native Transnistria under the authorization of the Rumanian government to report on the religious situation. If there was question of Glaser becoming a bishop or apostolic administrator, concluded the cardinal with strong irony, it was not for Berlin to "offer" it.

The Maier-Hultchin manuscript, censored by the British, never appeared. It illustrates, nevertheless, the compulsion of even knowledgeable observers to believe seriously in such a caricature of Nazi-Vatican relations, naïvely attributing to Hitler a benevolent yearning to save Christianity in Russia.

The rumors of such unholy tractations caused uneasiness and alarm in exile Russian circles. Helena Isvolsky, daughter of a famous Czarist diplomat, confided her fears to the Catholic, lay-edited, weekly review *Commonweal* (New York) in the issue of February 19, 1943. She wrote about life in Russia under the Nazis. Her principal source was the information bulletin of the International Commission Pro-Deo, located in Geneva and published by the brothers Lodygensky. They warned (October 1941) of the perils of competition among Protestants, Catholics, and Orthodox in the future Russia.

Isvolsky took a serious view of possible damage to mutual relations: "Yet there have been rumors of Catholic priests (both of the Latin and the Eastern rite) brought by the Germans to occupied Russia." She admitted these were only rumors. "Even so, it is unfortunate that statements have been made, and it is a fact that long before the Lodygenskys' report, similar assertions reached us from various sources. The very fact of Catholic missionaries being sponsored by the Nazis is enough to breed the worst kind of hostility and distrust. German interference can only discredit the Eastern Catholic rite in Russia for many years to come." It is the deplorable historical truth, she went on, that Catholic missionaries too often came to Russia with an invader.

"Catholic missionaries sponsored by the Nazis": she must have believed it herself to write in this way. No doubt she would have been happy to know the truth. One is aghast at the regrettable lack of knowledge, in those days, of the real state of affairs—and as late as 1943. Hitler, in this sense, did the ecumenical movement a great service by banning priests from going with the Germans into Russia. To borrow the writer's phrases, at least this time, thanks to the Führer, Catholic missionaries did not "come to Russia with the invader" but in spite of him.

What did the Soviet press say about all this? Curiously, the Soviets at first, in 1941, had no interest in charging that the Vatican and Berlin were hand in glove in invading the country. The propaganda tended rather piously to identify Hitler with the anti-Christ. The clandestine Comintern radio *Der Christliche Sender* hammered home the anti-Christian intentions of the National Socialists. In the desperate situation, it called on its listeners to "resist the anti-Christ". It was only in 1944 that a harsh anti-Vatican tone was heard. With the Red Army penetrating traditional Catholic countries, the new propaganda began to get up steam. In the autumn of that year, the Soviet magazine *War and the Working Class,* with an article signed simply "D. Petrov", brought up the Packard article cited above. "The article", reported the *New York Times* of October 10, 1944, "quoted an American magazine article of January 1943, by a former United Press correspondent in Rome which said that the Vatican had prepared and sent many priests into German-occupied parts of the Soviet Union, after instructing them 'how to struggle against heretical ideas spread by leaders of the Soviet state'." Petrov wrote further that the Germans "vainly hoped to use these Catholic priests for controlling the Russians and reconciling them to German occupation".

Neither in this article nor in any other appearing later did Soviet spokesmen adduce facts other than those they derived from clippings out of the foreign press. The "Petrov" story was repeated by M. M. Sheinman, a propagandist specializing in anti-God themes. In compiling his information on this occasion, he cited the Packard article and the passing remark in the book of Gabriel Louis Jaray. In this book Sheinman copied information that had already appeared in the East German (Communist) newspapers, that the Superior General of the Jesuits, Polish-born Wladimir Ledochowski, in Rome had worked with German military to allow the Jesuits to go as missionaries in the Soviet Union. The result of this, wrote Sheinman, was a "special agreement" between the Vatican and the Hitler regime by which specially formed Vatican agents would be sent. The source of this story was a book by a Nazi intelligence officer under Himmler, Austrian-born Wilhelm Hoettl. He did indeed seek some kind of cooperation with the Catholic Church in the person of the Jesuit priest. Hoettl's unauthorized initiative came to naught and outraged his SS superiors, who disciplined him. In any case, in his book mentioned by Sheinman, Hoettl made no mention of priests going to Russia. That was left to the fancy of the Moscow writer. In an earlier book, *The Vatican between the Two Wars,* first issued in Russian in 1948, Sheinman tells us that the Gabriel Louis Jaray quote had been used by *Pravda* of February 28, 1946, in an article by one I. Borisov. We read this formulation of the Kremlin's propaganda:

> This [the Packard article], it is to be noted, was not written by the adversaries of clericalism but by ardent partisans of the Vatican. They testify that the Nazi brigands brought Vatican agents along with them. The Vatican thought thereby to be able not only to destroy Communism but also, with the help of Hitler, to reach its long-standing objective of converting to Catholicism the people of the Soviet Union. Hence it was delighted with the prospect that seemed likely of the defeat of the Soviet state. That is why it was silent while the Nazi bands made rivers of blood flow.

This is Soviet anti-Vatican propaganda in its characteristic expression. From a Soviet propagandist we can turn to a Soviet historian, but with hardly better results: G. Déborine's *La Deuxième Guerre Mondiale. Étude politique et militaire.* The writer makes the following digest of all the previous allegations—which he presents as the unquestionable truth:

> The Pope, notified in advance [*sic*] by Germany of its plans, obliged the clergy to launch a great anti-Soviet campaign and to demand active aid to the Hitlerians. The Vatican and Germany had concluded an agreement. The Vatican would send into the Soviet territory, with the German army, agents for implanting

Catholicism, so that the occupants could subject the Soviet peoples and organize espionage and sabotage.

The only source given is the book *The Catholic Church against the Twentieth Century,* by Avro Manhattan of London, a well-known rationalist pamphleteer of the old school. (Of course the Pope was not "notified in advance by the Germans".) Truth to tell, it was not solely Communist or similar publications that took up the convenient quotes from Gabriel Louis Jaray. The French Jesuit Paul Duclos in his thesis *Le Vatican et la Seconde Guerre Mondiale* himself accepted it without question. He used it as basis for the affirmation that Hitler had authorized Catholic priests to go to the occupied regions. This lapse of critical sense must be attributed to haste in meeting the deadline for the defense of a doctoral work.

The nonhistory of the hallucinating "secret pact" between Hitler and Pius XII went on in other places much after the war. An obscure, one-man agency with the high-sounding name of Archiv zur Zeitgeschichte, edited out of Leonburg-Stuttgart, in 1958 published what it alleged to be documentary proof of the aid given to Catholic priests by the Wehrmacht, on orders from Berlin. According to the bulletin of the Archiv, entitled *Informationsdienst,* at least two army orders indicate military backing for religious work in Russia. (The *Archiv,* by the way, is not to be confused with the Institut für Zeitgeschichte of Munich or with its review *Vierteljahrshefte für Zeitgeschichte.*)

The person who edited the *Informationsdienst* was one Alfred Miller, an early National Socialist. He at one time worked for the newspaper *Völkischer Beobachter* of Alfred Rosenberg while writing anticlerical books. This pronouncedly individualistic Swabian broke with Rosenberg and the party and indeed for a time was confined to the Buchenwald concentration camp. But his ingrained anticlericalism remained with him to find a new outlet after the war.

Astonishingly, the two army orders turn out on scrutiny to be the very same Keitel orders alluded to here and cited more fully in the next chapter, in which it is clear that, far from favoring religious action, the military were ordered to keep a distance and particularly not to invite or permit any civilian priests to come from the outside. How did Alfred Miller manage to turn it around to mean the exact opposite? He did not print the whole texts, but only a few phrases to which he put a different twist, impressive for the reader who would not know any better. Miller's bitter anticlericalism, of which this and other bulletins of his give ample witness, overcame him.

Fraud or not, Miller could congratulate himself on his success. He was enthusiastically quoted, for instance, by Hubert Mohr, in his anti-Catholic attack published in the then German Democratic Republic in 1965, *Katholische Kirche und deutscher Imperialismus.* A feather in his cap was the use made of his material by Eduard Winter, a supposedly reputable historian in Communist Germany. Professor Winter of the East Berlin Wilhelm Humboldt University had to his credit a series of scholarly historical works, mostly on questions dealing with Eastern Europe. At a symposium on the theme of "German imperialism" held in Berlin in 1959, he read a paper called "The Vatican and German Imperialism in the Second World War". The proceedings were later published. Winter had been a priest of the Moravian diocese of Olomuc, professor at the Charles University in Prague, and active in student movements. He was caught up in the nationalist fervor of Sudeten youth before the war. He abandoned his priestly calling in 1940, continuing his professorship in the Nazi protectorate under Reinhard Heydrich. After the war he was taken on at Humboldt University by the Communists, who were able to close their eyes to his past political history.

In the Berlin symposium Winter chose to rely on Alfred Miller's *Informationsdienst,* with all its manipulated documentation on priests going to Russia with Hitler's approval. He made no visible effort to go beyond Miller's truncated quotes, nor were there any signs of independent research on the subject. One had a right to expect more from a qualified scholar with his own means to find out for himself.

How is it explained that the legend, the lie, of a Berlin-Vatican entente persisted for so long and in such various manifestations? Communist propaganda undoubtedly contributed chiefly, but this in turn could rely on the receptivity, even the bigotry, betraying itself too often in the world of democratic journalism. They believed it because they wanted to believe it. It was a handy weapon with which to attack the Catholic Church in the post-war years: Vatican collaboration with the Nazis.

Catholic priests did want to go to Russia, and they did go. But Hitler did all he could to stop them. The story of the Nazi Reich's intensive effort to block the Vatican and why is the subject of the next chapter.

Chapter 13

HOW AND WHY HITLER BLOCKED
THE VATICAN IN RUSSIA

In Ukraine, in June 1941, the Wehrmacht troops were welcomed as liberators. The local priest met them with the traditional honors to distinguished visitors, offering bread and salt. In the first days German propaganda for foreign use announced religion would be respected—welcome news for a people that had suffered under Bolshevik atheism for decades. The German radio (Zeesen) on June 22, in Russian and Ukrainian, promised religious freedom: "One of the first measures of the German administration will be the restoration of freedom for religion. We Germans are of a different faith from you, but we respect every honest religious conviction. We will allow you to organize your parishes." In retrospect, this was a very ambiguous pledge. In the Reich, some newspapers managed to carry stories and publish pictures of churches repaired and restored to sacred use after having been profaned for years as godless museums, granaries, or nightclubs. Other pictures displayed German soldiers in a march-by under the benediction of a priest robed in sacerdotal vestments. It was very good propaganda, one would think, but not the kind that the National Socialists had in mind. It did not last very long, especially after Dr. Goebbels realized that it could have a bad effect on the people at home. In fact, Hitler himself issued an order through Martin Bormann on November 14, 1941, expressing the wish that "until further notice nothing should be published about the religious situation in the Soviet Union". In a later communication to the Foreign Ministry Bormann explained, after consulting with Hitler, that this did not apply to propaganda abroad, for instance, in Sweden.

On July 16, when the war seemed to be going well, Hitler called in his closest aides—Rosenberg, Bormann, Lammers, Keitel, Göring, and others—for a review of the plans prepared for administering the newly acquired territories. For one thing he emphatically ruled out religious work by clergy coming from the outside, meaning, above all, sent by the Vatican. Several participants duly recorded Hitler's outburst on that day. One (possibly Bormann) wrote, "Incidentally, the Führer emphasizes that activities on the part of the churches are out of the question. Papen had sent him through the Foreign Ministry a long memorandum in which it was asserted now was the right moment to reestablish the churches, but this was completely out of the question." Another note, by Counselor Hasso von Etzdorf of the Foreign Ministry, is dated July 17, the following day:

> Papen has proposed to the Führer that Russia be led back to Christianity in order to strengthen morale. Führer: idea of the "old jockey" [on] missionary activity was entirely out of the question. If one did it at all, one should permit all the Christian denominations to enter Russia in order that they club each other to death with their crucifixes.

A third independent record of the event is found more amply in the diary of Dr. Otto von Bräutigam, who was an assistant to Rosenberg:

> Besides, he [Hitler] sharply criticized Ambassador von Papen, who had submitted a plan for religious missionary activity in the occupied territories, apparently through Rome. The Führer took this proposal badly and expressly forbade any religious influence in the country from the outside. On second thought, he wondered whether he should not have opened the door to all Christian denominations; in all probability they would then proceed to bash each other's heads in with their crucifixes. But then the Führer doubted the clergy's taste for self-sacrifice

and its eagerness for martyrdom. In this respect, he said, experiences in Spain had been disappointing. Nowadays, he continued, it was the fanatical Communists rather than the clergy who were prepared to die for their convictions.

What Franz von Papen, ex-vice-chancellor and currently ambassador in Turkey, really proposed has not come down in the record, but he himself in a written declaration years later (April 25, 1964) explained:

> Most certainly I never submitted to Hitler a scheme for conducting missionary work—"apparently through Rome"—in the occupied Soviet provinces. Probably Hitler confused it with a suggestion I had submitted to him in 1941 "to open again all the churches in the towns and villages of the then occupied areas, for the many people who eagerly wanted religious liberty". I was told later that this proposition had met with the vehement opposition of Rosenberg.

From the beginning, therefore, it was the explicit will of Hitler to exclude the Christian denominations in Germany or elsewhere, above all Rome, from any possibility of action in the old Soviet Union, now reeling under the onslaught of the German forces. The initial reports by correspondents with the troops tending to play up the revival of religious life with German help disappeared from the newspapers and radio. Hitler's words of July 16 were an expression of policy. Alfred Rosenberg (later hanged at Nuremberg) was made head of the new Ostministerium, or Eastern Ministry. He was the last man in the world to wish to encourage religious activity. He early notified the Foreign Ministry that the entry of church representatives into the area was banned. But Reinhard Heydrich, chief of the Reich Main Security Office, or Reichssicherheitshauptamt (RSHA), outdid himself with long and vehement denunciations of alleged Vatican plans, or plots, to evangelize Russia with or without the help of the Nazis.

Heydrich, in short, did not delay putting flesh on Hitler's anti-Church program. In a notice to the Foreign Ministry dated

July 21, he wrote on the subject, "New tactics in Vatican Russia work." The Vatican, he said, had previously developed a line of action with regard to religious assistance in the Soviet Union. But now the recent events had brought a change. He called it the "Tisserant plan", after Cardinal Eugène Tisserant, head of the Vatican's Congregation for the Eastern Church. With the German-Soviet conflict, wrote Heydrich, the Vatican had advanced on a two-pronged project. The French-born Tisserant, known for his anti-German stands, had now issued directives that the entire Vatican-Russia policy be concentrated on the two Catholic Slavic states, Croatia and Slovakia, but especially the latter. A second channel, went on the RSHA chief, was based on the volunteer legions allied with the Reich, especially from Spain and Croatia, and likewise the combat units of Italy, Slovakia, and Hungary. According to the Vatican's intentions, these units would be furnished with as many military chaplains as possible. They would prepare the terrain for Vatican work and try to influence the Russian people. Also, they were "to study the country, in order to develop further plans for Vatican Russian work on the basis of the experiences of the chaplains". Clearly, the Tisserant plan was a fly in the ointment and even a threat to the confident conquerors of Bolshevism and therefore to be short-circuited if possible. One way to do this was to have the military commanders keep vigil on suspect presences.

That such a detailed intelligence survey was ready so soon after Hitler's meeting with Rosenberg and the others shows that the RSHA had been studying the possible reactions of the Holy See for some time, even long before the beginning of the war in Russia. We find an authentic expression of Heydrich's suspicious and hostile thinking in a contemporary analysis of the current situation of the Catholic Church from the police point of view. Dated only July 1941 and intended for internal RSHA use, it concluded succinctly, "It is necessary to prevent Catholicism from becoming the real beneficiary of the war in the new situation that is developing in the Russian area conquered by German blood."

The bureaucratic process took its course. The military commanders were soon brought into line. The early weeks had shown that the local army authorities were not informed of the mind of the Führer when they so lightly engaged in religious propaganda with their spectacular "opening" of the churches. The indiscreet attention accorded to the local population irritated Berlin. Soon precise orders came their way from the High Command (OKW) in the form of a *Führerbefehl,* or express order of Hitler. In brief, the military were admonished to abstain from involvement in such things as the rehabilitation of churches or in allowing joint religious services. The chaplains were not to engage in religious work among the civilian population. The order stipulated, more significantly, that the commanders were not to allow or invite priests from the "outside" to enter their zone.

This remarkable top-level order from Hitler himself was decisive for the religious history of the German occupation of Russia in these months. There were two successive orders. The first is dated August 6, and the second, a supplement, is dated October 6. Both were signed in Hitler's name by Wilhelm Keitel, as chief of the High Command of the Armed Forces (*Chef OKW*), who was later hanged at Nuremberg. The order of August 8 runs as follows:

> The Führer has given the following directives concerning the conduct of the Wehrmacht in religious questions relating to the civil population of the newly occupied East Zone:
>
> 1. Religious or church activity of the civilian population is to be neither promoted nor hindered. Wehrmacht members are absolutely to hold themselves aloof from such manifestations of the indigenous people.
>
> 2. Wehrmacht religious work is exclusively destined for members of the Wehrmacht. Wehrmacht chaplains are to be expressly forbidden to engage in any kind of church or religious propaganda among the civilian population.
>
> 3. It is further forbidden to permit or to invite into the East Zone civilian clergy from the Reich or from abroad.

4. This directive does not apply to the Bessarabia zone occupied by the Rumanian troops, or to the Finnish front.

Hitler thought he was not sufficiently clear in his ban on religious contacts of the military with the local population. He was still afraid that the chaplains, especially those of the non-German units (Italians, Spanish, Hungarians, Slovaks, and others) might circumvent his peremptory orders. A lower-level (army) order of September 4 compliantly instructed commanders to report to the High Command of the Army (OKH) any special "signs of the activating of Vatican Russian work". This was not enough for the confident Führer, and he therefore elaborated with an additional *Führerbefehl* dated October 6. We can summarize: (1) If there are any army church services in the occupied zone, they must be held as field services and never in former Russian churches. Also, the local population is not to take part in the military services. (2) Churches destroyed by the Soviets or in war action are not to be repaired or returned to their original purposes by elements of the Wehrmacht. This is to be left to the civilian Russian population. The order was to be made known to all units down to company level. Units that had chaplains attached to them were required to inform said chaplains of the order with utmost dispatch and were to secure written acknowledgment, which was to be put in their record.

On the face of it, these orders seem merely to say that the army should attend to its own affairs and not get mixed up in the problems of the locals. But why a special order for the religious side of life in Russia? The first answer is that in fact the military had taken too enthusiastically to the idea of the "crusade" and had succumbed in the first days to the appeals of the civilians for help at least in reopening (restoring) their profaned churches. The second is that, as revealed in Heydrich's intelligence report already cited, there reigned in the Nazi mind the nightmare that the military forces might serve as a means of infiltration by the Vatican. The order was ideologically motivated.

The High Command felt that it owed an explanation to its

generals. A week after the first order we find its communication dated August 14 expounding the Tisserant plan. It was a summary of the same Heydrich intelligence report of July 21.

In the final analysis it was not the RSHA or the Wehrmacht but Rosenberg's Ostministerium that had in its hand religious life in the newly acquired Russian areas. Rosenberg had his share in framing the exclusion policy, if he was not its originator. Before the June 22 attack he and his collaborators were busy preparing their program—how to organize their new domain, for instance, the collective farming system. He had also to address the more delicate question of religious policy. We are informed of this phase of Nazi occupation planning by Otto von Bräutigam. In his diary he relates that he himself was given the task of drawing up a draft decree on religion. The general thrust was "toleration", that is, as far as the Nazis understood the word. The support of the people was to be won over in this way. However, he relates, Rosenberg and his entourage were aware how National Socialism had fought the Catholic and Evangelical confessions in Germany, and the doubt arose that the Germans at home would get a "negative impression" of (that is, would scoff at) an edict on "toleration" bearing the name of the author of *The Myth of the Twentieth Century.* Bräutigam had to lament that the decree eventually decided was never in fact made public and its propaganda scope was therefore nullified.

In the "toleration edict" no special preference was to be given to any particular confession, provided that the clergy stayed out of political activity. Church buildings were to be restored to their former owners. The decree did not even exclude Jews, and they would therefore also get their synagogues back. (One can imagine what this meant in practice.) But Rosenberg did not want any Catholic priests to come from the outside. As Bräutigam wrote, in Rome there existed an institute for preparing priests to go to Russia. Coming to the question of priests from the outside, Bräutigam dared to propose an exception: at least priests who had lived in Ukraine or along the Volga could return for religious work with the German communities, long established in those regions. But when this was presented, Rosenberg blue-penciled it. Not even German nationals originating in Ukraine (like Bräutigam himself) could be admitted back, in the case that they were priests. Evidently Rosenberg and Hitler could have no peace until every possible loophole was closed against the Vatican infiltration about which they were so nervous.

The military orders applied also to the Italian units operating in Russia, but this proved to be more difficult of realization. Heydrich was infuriated when he learned that in Italy public collections—for example, by the Milan Catholic daily, *L'Italia,* were taken up for reconstruction of churches and for the printing of holy cards and prayer books. And who were to distribute them? Naturally, the soldiers of the Italian expeditionary force. This was an open breach in the solid wall erected to block Catholic religious work in atheist Russia. The Italian commanders did not take very energetic measures to suppress this traffic. The SS of Reinhard Heydrich were unable to prevent a simple Italian soldier from giving a Madonna icon to a child. This happened in September 1941. But as of July 4, 1942, we find Erich Koch, Rosenberg's subordinate as Reichskommisar for Ukraine, denouncing the indiscipline of their allies. The Hungarians and Slovaks openly disregarded the prohibitions. They should be admonished. "Because the spread of Roman Catholicism is fundamentally undesirable and seems dangerous, I ask that the allied powers be asked to indicate to their military chaplains to limit themselves solely to work for the troops. I recommend also that the Italian leadership be informed of this viewpoint."

What also infuriated Heydrich were reports of an agreement imminent, or even already in force, between the Vatican and the Reich government on joint work in Russia. As far as the RSHA chief was concerned, these rumors—quite baseless—were planted by the Vatican itself to force Berlin into some kind of accommodation. In the meantime, he grumbled, the Vatican was going ahead anyway.

What more could be done to counter the Tisserant plan? In the coming long months political necessities forced some relaxation of the general ban on outside clergy in the occupied areas. In the beginning of 1943, Martin Bormann, secretary of the party chancery, with immediate and daily access to Hitler, accused Rosenberg himself of departing from the exclusion policy expressed on July 16, 1941. The head of the Ostministerium replied indignantly that it had never occurred to him to consider the old policy as a dead letter. He admitted that there were exceptional circumstances sometimes. He reminded Bormann that Himmler himself had allowed preachers from Transylvania to work among the German population (*Volksdeutsche*) in the neighboring German-occupied territories. He wrote also that Himmler allowed the Mennonites to send lay preachers to Ukraine. He admitted that he, too, had allowed some clerics to return to their own origins, but certainly not Catholic priests. He argued that the local *Volksdeutsche* should not be left to have their contact first with Wehrmacht chaplains before the party had a chance to present its own spokesman. But the admission of Catholic priests, he insisted, was out of the question. "In a special way," he protested to Bormann and, of course, through him to Hitler, as proof of his fidelity, "it is absolutely necessary to keep out the Catholic priests." The Nazi Reich was already crumbling, but the old ideology remained intact.

Chapter 14

EVANGELIZATION IN RUSSIA: THE REAL STORY

How could the so-called Tisserant plan cause such nervousness in Nazi ranks, from Hitler down? The phantom of a Vatican-controlled army of priests crossing over the borders into Russia was indeed highly unsettling. The ban, conceived as a means of choking the effort, was a natural expression of their habitual antipapal policy at home in Germany. But a new motivation was in play: two contrasting conceptions of "anti-Bolshevism", the religious and the political, hence Hitler's determination, even before the June attack, to exclude the Catholic Church from any part of the new enterprise. Add the thoroughness of a totalitarian system, and you see the relentless tracking down of every little priest who managed to cross into Russia in order to help his neighbors, deprived for decades of the consolations of religion. This was already too much, as far as the police were concerned. It portended unwelcome Vatican influence in the "Eastern territories" they were determined to hold, unshared.

There was, indeed, a "plan"—not of Cardinal Tisserant but of the Holy See—to come to the assistance of Catholics persecuted in the Soviet Union. The desperate efforts, notably of Pius XI, whose pontificate (1922–39) spanned the growth of the Communist danger, form a dramatic chapter in the history of the Catholic Church in this century. Alarm for the state of religion in the godless Soviet Union long antedated the war. Pius XI failed to reach even a minimum accommodation with Moscow. On the contrary, the Soviet antireligious campaign became ever more intense, of which the Catholic Church was not the only victim. The Orthodox Church suffered even more, if that was any consolation for Catholics. Unashamed anti-God propaganda became ever more violent and crude. Was religion at an end in Holy Russia?

It took decades before it was evident that all the propaganda and state power had failed to root out belief from the Russian soul. But that was not so obvious in the 1920s or the 1930s. In the end, the very intensity of the campaign only proved the opposite of what was intended. But for years after the Bolshevik Revolution of 1917 the Holy See encountered successive defeats. Disaster followed on disaster. A show trial of leading Catholic figures in Moscow in 1923 gave world opinion a first view of the impious, persecuting intent of the Bolsheviks. Soon all the bishops of the Latin rite—such as they were—had been exiled, imprisoned, or shot. The Holy See did not, however, interrupt contacts. The apostolic nuncio in Berlin, Archbishop Eugenio Pacelli, the future Pius XII, negotiated with Soviet diplomats up to as late as 1927 in search of a formula. Nothing came of it. In 1925 Pius XI decided on a drastic approach. The French Jesuit Michel d'Herbigny, who was at that time rector of the Pontifical Oriental Institute in Rome, was sent on a mission secretly to ordain as bishops a half-dozen priests. He was himself ordained bishop in Berlin, by Archbishop Pacelli, en route to Moscow. The ordinations took place in secret, but the secret could not be maintained. All or nearly all of the clandestine bishops were eliminated, in one way or another. The enterprise was a humiliating failure. In the end of the 1920s Joseph Stalin consolidated his personal hold on the levers of power without the least relaxation of antireligious policy.

In April 1929 Pius XI created a special Vatican "Commission for Russia". Later that year he erected the "Pontifical Russian College", better known as the "Russicum". Its mission was to educate young clerical students (of any nationality) for service in Russia, when the doors should open—and in fact, even without waiting. At the same time he inaugurated the Pontifical Ruthenian College for Ukrainians. The Russicum was under the direction of the Jesuits, whose superior general, Ledochowski, a Pole, took an intense interest in its development. Pius XI also invited other religious communities to prepare their own apostolic workers. In mid-1941 Heydrich could list some of these, in addition to the two already named. They were the Abbey of Grottaferrata just outside of Rome, the Abbey of Chevetogne in Belgium, and the Abbey of Velehrad in Moravia. In addition, the Redemptorists, Assumptionists, and other communities, according to the Pope's wishes, had their own program. In Poland, where there was a natural interest, and not only because it once was part of the Czarist Empire, a similar zeal was manifest. The movement Oriens was particularly involved. Many Polish priests of the older generation had studied in Saint Petersburg (Leningrad) and wanted nothing better than to return there. Finally, under date of February 2, 1930, Pius XI addressed a public letter to the cardinal vicar of Rome ordering him to organize a service of propitiation in Saint Peter's and to pray for Russia. He welcomed similar ceremonies elsewhere in the Catholic world. He recited gravely the long history of his efforts in behalf of the people of Russia — the Vatican's aid for the famine victims, the papal intervention in favor of the Orthodox Patriarch Tykhon, the futile negotiations with various Soviet diplomats. (He did not mention the disastrous d'Herbigny experiment.) The papal letter was a cry of desperation. It touched off a new phase of Vatican evangelization in Russia. The Tisserant plan was launched.

The arduous Russian mission, with its risks, even the risk of death, had precedents in Church history. One can recall the martyrdom of the many priests educated at the English (and Scots) College in Rome (and elsewhere on the Continent) who smuggled themselves into England during the Elizabethan persecutions, to endure atrocious tortures and finally execution by being hanged, drawn, and quartered, as befitted traitors. We know of these martyrs because their trials, if cruel, were at least public. Those who went to Russia in clandestinity, before or after June 1941, had no such fortune. Even today the ultimate destiny of some ex-students of the Russicum is still shrouded in mystery. One of these was George Moskwa, a Pole, graduate of the Russicum. He slipped into Ukraine on the eve of the war. He was sent back to Rome in 1940 as a courier for the metropolitan of Lwow (Lviv), the venerable Andreas Sheptytsky. He set off from Rome to his post only to disappear en route. He was last seen in Budapest. Was he arrested and sent to Siberia to die unknown or simply shot outright?

A similar story of hardihood but with a happier ending was the experience of the American Jesuit Walter Ciszek, also a graduate of the Russicum. It can be said that he did not go to the Russians, but instead they came to him. He was on the Polish-Soviet frontier at Dubno, Poland, at a Jesuit house called the Albertyn, when the Red Army in September 1939 occupied that city. Faithful to his mission, he volunteered on the spot, after consulting Metropolitan Sheptytsky, for a Soviet labor battalion and arrived in the Urals. But he was already under surveillance, and when the Nazis attacked in June 1941 he was arrested. There followed five years in the infamous Lublianka prison in Moscow, accused of being a "Vatican spy", or in reverse, invited to spy for the NKVD. He was then sent for a ten-year stay at hard labor in Siberia, at Norilsk, near the Arctic Circle. He was given up for dead by his confreres and relatives. He could finally return to the United States in 1955 in an exchange for some Soviet spies arrested in the United States. What of the others, and how many were they? At the time discretion was the order of the day. Both the Soviets and the Nazis had their informers. The less that was said, the better. During the war itself communication was difficult in any case. After the war, with Soviet control in Eastern Europe, those in a position to know could not publish the story in any open fashion. Accounts that did emerge during or after the war are characterized—disappointingly for the chronicler—by generalities, without names, places, or means of verification. We have, for instance, in our hands the version of a Polish resister who admittedly was only a third-hand witness. According to him:

> When the German army advanced into Russian territory, news started coming from the Polish *Volksdeutsche* draftees that the Russians, once they got the feeling that a soldier was not quite so German as he appeared, started asking questions about Catholic priests. This prompted a group of young Polish priests who had managed to avoid arrest by the Gestapo to declare themselves civilian *Volksdeutsche* and to volunteer for the German army. Once in Russia they deserted and went to live with the Russian population.

The priests spent the nights hearing the confessions of those who had been without the sacraments for years. People who became aware that a priest was nearby flocked by the hundreds to his side. This was a dangerous situation, needless to say, and could only attract the attention of the police. If the Germans caught them they could be summarily shot as deserters; a like fate awaited them if they fell into the hands of the Soviets. In fact, we read in this account, "I do not know of any one of them who survived."

A more detailed account, possibly of the same origin, appeared in the immediate postwar years. This concerned the activity of one of the priests of Oriens, the Polish work already mentioned. We can summarize:

> The German Transport Command in Russia needed grooms to take care of its horses and recruited Poles for this purpose. The priest seized the opportunity and went east, caring for horses and making contacts at every opportunity. He discovered that he was the first Catholic priest to visit any of the villages in nearly thirty years. While the majority of those living in the villages were Russian Orthodox, the priest discovered a remarkable number of Catholics. Once a contact had been made, the news that a priest was there spread with amazing swiftness. Usually he was able to make temporary headquarters in some barn, and there he received Catholics in large numbers who came during the night, bringing children to be baptized, seeking a religious wedding ceremony, making their confessions,

and begging to attend Mass and receive Holy Communion. Very early in the morning he would celebrate Mass, to be astonished at how many remembered the Latin sufficiently to make the responses.

An enlightening detail is that German priests, conscripted into the Wehrmacht, conspired to help the Polish priests in their ministry, themselves also doing pastoral work among the people despite the prohibitions. Again, we are without particulars. While there is no reason to doubt the general authenticity of the accounts, names and places as well as corroborating witness are lacking.

Was this the Tisserant plan that set the Nazis so much on edge? Not exactly. This would be to overlook and underestimate the religious tension built up along the Soviet border from the Baltics to the Black Sea in the years of persecution. The reaction of Catholics to the new opportunities in 1941 did not need any Vatican stimulus. The situation spoke for itself. Only a few miles away there were other Catholics absolutely cut off from religion, stripped of their own priests, robbed of their churches, which had been turned into warehouses or atheist museums. Many of them were Poles or Lithuanians settled in those areas (White Russia and Ukraine) for long years, since Czarist times. One reason why so little is known of this religious effort is that it was spontaneous, personal, voluntary, instinctive—leaving no formal record.

Fortunately, there are some names. On March 24, 1966, there died in his native Slovakia, at age eighty-four, one whose life and work corresponded authentically to the mission of the Russicum, the Jesuit Father Wendelin Javorka. He was the first rector (1929) of this Roman institute founded by Pius XI. Paradoxically, he never entered the "promised land". He promptly set off for Russia in 1941, going first to Slovakia. But his application to go farther, into the German-controlled zone, was refused. He incarnated in his person, as former rector of the Russicum, the Tisserant plan itself. In a few months he moved to Rumanian-controlled territory, to Cernauti in Bucovina, just retaken from the retreating

Red Army. It provided him ample opportunities for his apostolate. In 1944, when the Soviets returned, he was arrested and in a trial in Kiev was sentenced to seventeen years in Siberia as an "agent of a foreign power". In 1956 he was given an amnesty and expelled from the Soviet Union. He returned to Slovakia. Father Javorka, despite his age and his disabilities, was never able to continue to Rome because of the opposition of the then Communist government.

Others followed in the traces of Javorka, each with his own dramatic destiny, often enough death or Siberia. Among those who disappeared without a trace was the Dutch Jesuit John Peeperkorn. He was in Riga (Latvia) in 1941. On September 15 he headed for Minsk in White Russia, of course without leave of the Germans. He wrote to a Capuchin friend on August 18, "Wonderful and enough to move to tears how the Faith has survived. I am convinced more than ever that God's work in Russia awaits God's men." He wrote again on November 15, this time from Hermanovice, calling for others to join him. They should come, he said, with no other hope than Christian trust in God's Providence. He explained that, in practice, it was more useful to know Polish than Russian, but even without Polish one could manage: "What is important is that good priests be there; everything else will take care of itself." He said he had been in Rosica (in Russia proper). He heard confessions for some hours, led a procession, and gave a sermon, with Vespers. He recommended that priests should go to Minsk or Borisov. The latter city, he wrote, "has twenty thousand factory workers; the population is Catholic and, as I am told, were always good Catholics. Catholicism in White Russia, that is, the *sensus catholicus,* still lives, as I have been told, around Minsk and Borisov."

Nothing more is heard of Peeperkorn. His own Dutch confreres in 1947 listed him among their dead, with the statement that neither the day nor the place of his death was known.

In the meantime, waiting in Kaunas (Lithuania) and Riga (Latvia) to return to their old posts in Russia were Bishop Theophilus Matulanis (also known as Matulionis) and Bishop

Boleslas Sloskan (also known as Sloskans). The first had the title of auxiliary bishop to the apostolic administrator of Leningrad. The second was apostolic administrator of both Mohilev (Moscow) and Minsk. They had been secretly ordained bishops years before. Matulanis had been among the priests sentenced in the famous Moscow trials of 1923. He was destined to spend most of his life in Soviet prison camps, in successive periods. Both had been driven out of the country years earlier. A return to their canonical jurisdiction would have been the first thought, if the Nazis had any intention of helping the Catholic Church in Russia. Well-known victims of Bolshevism, they could not be easily objected to from the political point of view. Sloskan never saw Russia again; Matulanis did, but on his way to Siberia, again, after the war.

Slovakia was another country with easy access to the Soviet Union. This sector, too, has been little studied. We know only a few cases. One was John Kellner, a Russicum student. He was able to work in Russia and did come back, only to be tried later by a Slovak Communist tribunal. Another Slovak was Michael Inhass. We know of his case because, after having circulated throughout Russia and returning to his native country, he emigrated to the United States, where he wrote a book on his experiences under the name "L. M. Telepun". The anonymous author was necessarily—and for the later chronicler, unfortunately —imprecise in his descriptions.

In Hungary and Rumania, where the German military did not have the final word, the situation was momentarily more favorable. Hungarian military chaplains took advantage of their situation to minister to the local civilian population. With the reoccupation of Bessarabia, Moldavia, and Bucovina by Rumania, priests could pass over the frontier. The chaplain of the German community in Bucharest, Nicholas Pieger, was able to go there and minister to the local German population. He was later joined by another German priest, Walter Kampe, later auxiliary bishop of Limburg, Germany. When the Germans got wind of their presence, they were ordered out of the zone. In the unique instance where the

Holy See could send one of its representatives, Bishop Mark Glaser, who was rector of the seminary at Jasy in Rumania, went to Transnistria (his place of origin) to survey the situation. It should be added that in 1940, after this area had passed to Soviet control, Berlin arranged for the evacuation of a dozen "Ruthenian" priests, that is, Ukrainians of the Eastern rite, as Germans, to Germany. In 1941–42 their requests to return were refused. They were reckoned among the "outside priests" whom Hitler did not want at any price to go to Russia.

As far as the German police were concerned, the finger of suspicion pointed chiefly at the chaplains of the military forces allied with Germany—the Italians, Spanish, Slovaks, Hungarians, and Croatians. They believed that the ranks of the chaplains were being artificially inflated as a cover for priests destined to evangelize Russia. The Nazis were not entirely wrong, even though they overestimated the proportions. There are at least two well-documented cases of Italian priests who got themselves taken on as military chaplains, with the ultimate objective of pursuing their vocation of religious work in Russia. These were the Jesuits Pietro Leoni and Pietro Alagiagian. Leoni had studied at the Russicum. He went as a chaplain on various fronts—Albania, Yugoslavia, Greece, and finally Russia. While exercising his priestly ministry with the troops, he also dedicated himself to work with the local population, especially in Ukraine—against German orders, of course. His Italian commanders closed their eyes. In 1943 he was able to return to Italy but immediately asked to be sent to Odessa. Mussolini had fallen. Leoni received a passport from the new Badoglio government and deliberately walked into the lion's den. Odessa was sure to fall to the Red Army soon, but it made no difference. All the better. Once in Odessa he could shift for himself, come what may. He was released from Siberia in 1955.

Alagiagian was much older and a real veteran of the Russian apostolate. He was born in Russian Armenia of Armenian-Italian origin. He had circulated in the Soviet Union from the Bolshevik Revolution, arrested many times. He became a chaplain late, departing only in 1942, after receiving the blessing of Pope Pius

XII for his mission. He was released from Siberia in 1954 as an Italian citizen.

Hitler and the Nazis did not make any distinction between Catholics of the Latin rite and those of the Eastern or Oriental or Byzantine rite. Yet as far as the Holy See and its policy toward the Eastern churches were concerned, this is a capital distinction. As has been seen, much of the religious work in White Russia was done by Latin rite priests, among Poles and Germans (*Volks-deutsche*). There were others, particularly from the Russicum, who were ordained in the Eastern rite and directed their efforts toward those in Russia of this rite. What Reinhard Heydrich nervously called the Tisserant plan betrayed ignorance of this distinction. It was a misnomer. Cardinal Eugène Tisserant was head (secretary) of the Pontifical Congregation for the Eastern Churches, that is, those varied populations that followed a rite other than the Latin. In particular, he was concerned with the Ukrainians. It was to him that the metropolitan of Lwow (Lviv), Andreas Sheptytsky, addressed himself. The "Latins" were not in Tisserant's competence. That would be to suppose that the Holy See wished to "Latinize" the peoples in Russia—Ukrainians or White Russians or Russians.

For these years, therefore, it is highly pertinent to inquire more closely as to what the Tisserant plan really amounted to. His mission was to help the Eastern churches in union with the Pope, for example, in the formation of priests of that rite, by providing liturgical books and religious articles appropriate and customary. But the German ban on "outside priests" applied equally to the Ukrainians. In the Reich and elsewhere in Europe there were numerous Ukrainian priests, married or not, ready to return to their homeland for religious purposes. In Berlin, there was a Ukrainian prelate, Monsignor Peter Werhun, who had the title of apostolic visitator of the Ukrainians in Germany. He was able, in the first weeks, to get to his homeland briefly and join in the euphoria of false hopes. But this was a good fortune he could not repeat. (In 1945 the Soviets scooped him up in Berlin; he died in Siberia a few years later.) He was unable to dispatch anyone to

Ukraine, unless there were exceptional cases of which we know nothing.

From Rome, Tisserant was able to dispatch some priests or clerics (deacons) to Ukraine as interpreters for the Italian army. Monks of the Order of Saint Basil, founded, or resurrected, by Sheptytsky himself, constituted the backbone of this group. Under his jurisdiction were also graduates of the Russicum, such as Leoni, Alagiagian, Moskwa, and Ciszek. The cardinal in later years made no secret of the fact that he had sent, in the name of the Holy See, eight apostolic workers to Russia, of whom four were Basilians and four were diocesan clergy, some of them deacons.

In the early months of the Soviet-German war, the cardinal, in his characteristic frank style, lifted the veil somewhat on his intentions in Russia (the real Tisserant plan). In a letter dated August 21, 1941, to the British minister to the Holy See, d'Arcy Osborne (who reported on this to his government), he wrote:

> We have only a small number of priests, practically all of Russian origin. In addition to some secular priests, we have some religious who have received a formation like that of the former students of the Russicum. Among them are a number of Slavic origin—Czechs or Slovaks in particular. At this moment we are printing for their use liturgical books in Slavic, according to the purest Russian traditions, and three of these are already on sale.

This was the "army" that gave such alarm to Hitler and Himmler in 1941.

Chapter 15

AFTER STALINGRAD: THE REICH
AS "BULWARK" OF EUROPE

The disaster at Stalingrad was a fateful political as well as military setback for Hitler. The capitulation of Field Marshal Friedrich von Paulus and his Sixth Army on February 2, 1943, cost the Reich several hundred thousand of its best soldiers. But it was also a blow to the mythical invincibility of the Wehrmacht and, above all, to the leadership of Hitler himself. The specter of defeat and a Napoleonic retreat loomed before the Axis. The population at home was profoundly shaken by the news. It was, in fact, the beginning of the end. But what happened in the next two years?

Hitler tightened controls, and Dr. Goebbels embarked on a new propaganda campaign at home and abroad. He had a difficult task, with the military situation working against him. He was to play the anti-Bolshevik theme to the utmost, but this time in a defensive sense. A key objective in his new strategy was to sow distrust and division in enemy ranks, between the Anglo-Americans and the Soviets, alternating hints of a separate peace, now with the one and now with the other. But above all, he hung before his public the image of Europe fallen into the hands of the Bolsheviks if the front did not hold. It was the greatest, and the last, propaganda campaign of Dr. Josef Goebbels.

In a speech on the anniversary of the *Machtergreifung,* or coming to power of the Nazis, on January 30 (it was read for him by Goebbels at the Sportpalast), Hitler had already outlined the new strategy, as the shadow of Stalingrad assumed its nightmarish shape. It was a grim bid for peace, but of course on German terms: "In this war there will be neither conqueror nor conquered, only the survivors and the dead." That is, he would pull down all Europe if he had to. It was also an implicit call to the West to take up the struggle against "Asiatic barbarism". But the propaganda drive was really opened by Goebbels from his usual rostrum in the Sportpalast on February 18, before his fanatical and enthusiastic adherents. He called for "total war" and sounded anew the warning of the Bolshevik danger, now so close to home.

In his diary, Goebbels recorded his immense satisfaction at the impact of his new campaign. On March 4 he noted, "Its echo has been extraordinary in the whole world. No speech during the whole war in Germany has been so vividly cited and commented on in the globe as the Sportpalast speech of February 18. It still dominates the headlines of the major newspapers in all the countries of the earth."

Some clippings on which Goebbels based his enthusiasm have survived in archives of the Propaganda Ministry, found in part today at the Yiddish Scientific Institute (YIVO), New York. They enlighten us on the sources Goebbels relied on for his optimism. Swiss papers dominate. They are *Le Journal de Genève, La Tribune,* and *La Suisse* of Geneva; and *La Feuille d'Avis, Il Gazette,* and *La Revue* of Lausanne. The *Journal* paraphrased Goebbels approvingly as saying, "That the West is threatened by a fearful danger is supported by logic and the facts."

On March 16 Goebbels held a reception for the foreign press, and the *Gazette* of Lausanne subsequently stressed his thesis: "For Europe there is only one choice: either the Axis or Bolshevism." A few days later, in the March 20 issue of *Das Reich,* his own publication, the propaganda minister hinted at a drive for splitting the enemy alliance when he wrote, "The decision faces us in the East, and not only for us but also for London and Washington." He also said that the British and the Americans could not of course speak their minds about the Bolshevik peril as openly as could the Axis.

A Goebbels aide, Rudolf Semmler, put this notation in his own diary for March 14: "In the past few weeks Goebbels has been trying to spread a feeling of panic throughout Europe by arousing fear of the Soviet armies. . . . He is already talking of open distrust between the Russians and their allies. Every shrewd observer, he is saying, can see the evidence of this growing tension, and it is a short step from open distrust to an open break." Czech President Edward Benes wrote to the same effect that from the spring of 1943 "propaganda against the so-called danger of Bolshevism and for the so-called saviors of civilization from the Soviet Union was continually stepped up with increasing vigor."

For their part, the Anglo-American propaganda services ignored or censored these ploys of Goebbels for fear of playing into his hands. In Vichy France the new atmosphere was graphically described in the diary of an acute observer whose business as a labor consultant made it possible for him to journey between Vichy and Paris and to contact officials, both German and French, in both places. He was Pierre Nicolle, who published his extensive notes after the war. On February 14, 1943—and therefore even before the speech at the Sportpalast—he recorded that Swiss journalists in Vichy told him how much their newspapers were concerned by the Communist threat and that many editorials were inspired by this fear. "The impression gathered in this milieu", wrote Nicolle, "is that it would not be surprising that a complete reversal of alliances might be brought about and a veritable crusade organized to stand in the way of Communism, with the Anglo-Saxons joining in this crusade." In a further note, of February 16, 1943, written after a visit to Paris, Nicolle wrote again:

In Paris, some very curious rumors circulate with persistence. There is talk of a possible overturn of alliances, that Germany is on the point of convincing the Americans and the English of the necessity to block jointly the Communist wave. . . . German circles stress the discourse of Goebbels, who describes Germany

as ready to double its efforts to strengthen the barrier raised
against Bolshevism. . . . The Communist danger, despite deeply
rooted anti-German feelings, is beginning to worry all the
provinces.

On March 4 Nicolle recorded that the Vichy Ministry of
Information, in its orientation for the press, had for some days
been devoted to the attitude of the English and the Americans
toward their Russian ally. "The orchestration", he commented,
"seems to have had excellent results: the Russian danger seen
through the American reactions gives pause to the critics of the
[Laval] government." On March 13, the writer continues, he had
seen a number of people convinced that diplomatic conversations
were already under way in various capitals and could lead to a
rapprochement between the Anglo-Saxons and the Germans, the
Russian peril being the basis of rapprochement. On March 20, he
noted that in Vichy certain diplomatic circles thought that the
first feelers for peace included the task of making the Americans
understand the necessity of retaining authoritarian government
in Italy and Germany, as alone capable of maintaining order, to
prevent a vast revolutionary and anarchist movement that would
be exploited by Communism. Hitler, or his party, would be in-
duced to proclaim that, after the peace, Germany would not try to
exercise political or economic hegemony over Europe but would
leave each country to determine its own form of government.

In this line, the diarist Pierre Nicolle also tells us about speculation on the visit of Archbishop Francis Spellman of New York to
Rome. It was linked to a simultaneous presence there of the Reich
foreign minister, Joachim von Ribbentrop. The U.S. prelate was
said to have met him. Was it to negotiate? It was open season for
political speculation by those desperately searching for a way
out.

Thus far for Western Europe. What about Eastern Europe and
its peoples, in the direct path of the Red Army? In new propaganda instructions of February 15, Goebbels cited Hitler's proclamation of January 30 and said that either Germany (and its allies

and therefore all Europe) must triumph, "or from the East, the inner-Asiatic, Bolshevistic tide will inundate the old culture-continent, in a way as destructive and annihilating as the fate of Russia itself". Accordingly, he argued, the defense of Europe was the mission of the East European peoples as well. Changes in policy were needed, he admitted. The populations needed to be treated differently. "We cannot call these men of the East, who look to us for liberation, beasts, barbarians, and so forth and then expect from them any concern for a German victory." Expressions like "colonies" or "object of booty" were therefore, he said, completely out of place.

Dr. Goebbels' problem was that it was already too late to ease matters by simply dictating a vocabulary change in the newspapers controlled by him. Could he not at least count on the spontaneous concern of these populations themselves? The allies of the Reich were indeed preoccupied, without any urging from Goebbels.

A propaganda official of Rosenberg's Eastern Ministry in a memo at this very time, February 23, warned that a negative argument would never get results. In addition to anti-Communist slogans, some new pledges to the peoples of the occupied countries were required. He referred not only to Eastern Europe but also to the occupied Western countries as well. He wrote:

> A solemn proclamation guaranteeing the future of the peoples of Europe would be in any case the decisive step that could lead to positive action by the European peoples. Our entire political and propagandistic effort in the occupied area habitually runs into difficulties because we cannot tell them anything about their future. The consequence of three or four years of waiting is only dissatisfaction.

This was to put the situation mildly and could be written at that time only by a Nazi official contemplating imminent collapse. The high leadership, that is, in practice, Hitler, had painted itself into a corner. The bankruptcy is illustrated by the pitiful propaganda directives issued at this time in Norway by Reich Commissar

Joseph Terboven: "Stress Communist danger; stop excessive attacks on Great Britain; stress German reverses and grave situation; don't speak of the certitude of German victory; recall with Goering that an accord is always possible with 'gentlemen' but never with the Bolsheviks."

In this way it was sought to prepare the ground for a separate peace with what was now being called the United Nations on the basis of a common front against the Soviets and on the basis, of course, of a National Socialist state ideologically and politically intact.

Such a development was not to be. Hitler was both unwilling and unable to reverse the course of ruthlessness that had served him so well up to then. He had few options. No word emanated from Berlin in the form of concessions to the national aspirations so profound in Eastern Europe. One clear sign of the immobilism of Hitler's policy and the inevitable consequences of past misdeeds was the failure of recruitment for a projected Lithuanian SS Legion for service on the Russian front. It had to be openly abandoned. In place of fighting men, the Nazis had to be content with forming labor battalions. In a statement issued on March 17, 1943, the Reich Commissar for Ostland, Hinrich Lohse, blamed the failure on "certain politically minded intellectual circles". The university was closed for this reason. "The persons responsible for such a state of affairs", he declared,

> stand condemned, not only before the European community but also before their own country, which, by its geographical location, is even more endangered by Bolshevism than Germany, which has mobilized all its forces for total war. The formation of the Lithuanian Legion is therefore abandoned. In the future, registration is to be continued only for labor needed for the army and for defense.

Early in 1944 the Germans allowed the formation instead of a "Lithuanian Territorial Corps" for internal defense. It had likewise to be disbanded because, it was said, of mutinies against its German officers.

A like Nazi-promoted "Polish Legion" was not seriously attempted. In early summer 1943, when decisions for a change—if any were to be made—would have been known to the Nazi satraps in the occupied Eastern territories, Hans Frank in Poland was still pleading with Berlin for adjustment to the realities. Writing to Hitler on June 19, as head of the "General Gouvernement" (Central Poland), he asked for a drastic revision of policy in order to win popular support against the Bolsheviks. A key factor to this end, he submitted, would be the Catholic clergy. He had to concede that the Church leaders had been the foremost supporters of the national movement, that is, anti-German, and that priests had been imprisoned and shot while Church property was confiscated. "However," he urged, "for winning the cooperation of the Polish population there is necessary if not the collaboration at least the loyal attitude of the Church." This reinforcement of the defensive front against Bolshevism, he thought, could be won without any doubt, especially under the impact of the Katyn forest revelations. The Poles, out of the instinct of sheer self-preservation, would have to oppose Bolshevik rule in the Vistula area. As one means for winning Church support, Frank urged that compensation be made for the confiscations. As an additional consideration he recalled the "extremely clever Bolshevik propaganda that during the occupation of Western Galicia [Ukraine] allowed the Catholic Church for propaganda reasons to continue her activity and retain her property".

A particularly pathetic incident in Poland dramatized the hopeless predicament of the Nazi occupants. It was the fiasco of "Operation Bertha", an unrealistic attempt to mobilize public opinion in Warsaw and elsewhere. In the first days of February 1944 the Goebbels office in Poland, headed by one Spengler, notified officials of the General Gouvernement (Central Poland) that they were to organize anti-Communist rallies in all key Polish and Ukrainian circles, for example, in the factories of Warsaw, Lublin, Radom, Lemberg (Lwow), Cracow, and so forth. This was to take place immediately over a period of three days, February 10–12, under the slogan "Popular European

Movement against Bolshevism". Similar rallies, it was said, had already been seen in White Russia, Estonia, Latvia, Lithuania, Denmark, Norway, France, Belgium, and so on, with calls for "the freedom of Europe".

A chorus of complaints arose in Nazi officialdom. The governor of Warsaw himself, Ludwig Fischer, wrote to Spengler on February 4 that he had not been consulted and that the project was absolutely unrealizable (*völlig undurchführbar*). The propaganda people, he said, had lost all contact with reality. Anyone rising to support the initiative in public was only condemning himself to death. "Any Pole who would do this is a candidate for death [*Todeskandidat*] because within twenty-four hours the Resistance would liquidate him." Fischer was unanimously supported by his colleagues. The hopeless "Operation Bertha" was dropped. Spengler turned to preparing booklets on the Red terror for distribution in the population. He was counting, with his chief in Berlin, on traditional Polish anti-Bolshevik sentiment. The timing was not in his favor.

Not even the Katyn story, though vigorously exploited, achieved Goebbels' ends. An unexpected propaganda key had come into his hands with the discovery, in the forest of Katyn outside of Smolensk, of the graves of thousands of Polish officers. On April 13, 1943, the German news agency DNB announced that ten thousand bodies had already been discovered, whose death went back to 1940, at the time of the Soviet occupation of Eastern Poland. The news was bread from heaven as far as Goebbels and Frank were concerned. The case was calculated to awaken all the deep-seated anti-Russian and anti-Bolshevik instincts among Poles. It profoundly shook the Polish government in London, which demanded an inquiry, convinced as they were that Stalin had ordered the massacre. They had long since sought in vain from Moscow the whereabouts of these officers, of whom nothing had been heard since 1940. In angry reaction, Stalin broke off diplomatic relations with the London Poles. Was it finally the break in the anti-Nazi coalition for which Goebbels was looking?

Frank's proposal for a simple compensation for confiscations was of course pitifully short of what was needed. At that moment, he could not ask for more from the Führer—and he did not get even this. Of a relaxation of the general anti-Church policy there could be no question, in Hitler's mind. It was not until April 5, 1944, that the archbishop of Cracow, Adam Sapieha, and Hans Frank met each other—for the first time in the whole course of the war. Hitler's representative asked for a more favorable attitude of the Church to the Nazis in the conflict with Russia. He must have known that after five years of Nazi occupation, the longest and the most brutal in record, a Bolshevik occupation could not have been worse. In any event Frank (hanged in Warsaw) got no satisfaction. Sapieha replied, according to Frank's own diary, that this was a political question and that he saw the situation "only as a man and as a bishop".

The slogan of Germany as the "bulwark" against Bolshevism meant only that the National Socialist regime and its works must survive. Two high Axis conferences at this phase leave no doubt of this. Foreign Minister Joachim von Ribbentrop was in Rome during February 24–28, 1943, with a large staff of advisers. The communique issued after his final meeting with Mussolini contained only one political note that could be interpreted as a serious gesture of reconciliation in the occupied countries, where control was rapidly slipping from Nazi hands. The manifesto, inspired by the Fascists, called for "the rights of nations and their free development". This short pronouncement meant everything and nothing. It was, however, blandly described by DNB, the German news agency, as the Magna Carta of the European continent. Its only importance was that it served as the point of departure for new peace rumors.

The Washington-based *Foreign Correspondence,* co-edited by Sir Wilmot Lewis and Edward Weintal, used by both the State Department and Whitehall to get useful information into circulation without committing themselves, said in its March 10 issue that Ribbentrop had "instructed" the Italians to emphasize the Bolshevik danger and to single out the Reich as the only bulwark. This is a case of informed speculation joined to subtle propaganda.

It was a good guess that Ribbentrop would have held that line with Mussolini. If so, he must have been sorely disappointed. From accounts now known, Mussolinian Italy at this stage was in fact seeking an honorable exit from the war as soon as possible. It needed no "instructions" from Berlin to stress the Communist danger. Plagued by internal difficulties, Italy had already withdrawn its decimated expeditionary force from Russia. The proposals for a liberalization in the East were its own.

Some weeks later, April 7–10, Hitler and Mussolini met in Vienna and there studied the bad situation as best they might. Again, the Italians pressed for a new policy calculated to win the support of the Eastern peoples. The Fascist government proposed an independence proclamation for Poland, the Baltic states, and Ukraine and an end to racial persecution. This was as if to expect the National Socialists to surrender all their war aims and their Nazi ideas. It is no surprise that Ribbentrop informed the Italians their suggestions were impossible.

Allied analysts noted with interest—and suspicion—broadcasts over Radio Roma by Giovanni Ansaldo and Aldo Valori, as also the editorials of Virginio Gayda in *Il Giornale d'Italia,* especially of February 17. Here it was proclaimed that all countries and all national governments, great and small, had the right to a free and independent existence. But these were Italian voices, and they did not speak for the Nazi Reich. When, in a few more months, Fascism had fallen, German propaganda was on its own—and no change in policy was in sight, unless it was the hope of dividing the Western democracies from their Soviet ally.

An American intelligence agency a year later pointed up the complete lack of any positive program effectively to rally the Eastern populations. It concluded: "Although all this is being done in conjunction with a running propaganda in the national-liberation line, the Germans have granted no real concessions in the direction of sovereignty. . . . Military necessity, the opposition bound up with the previous pattern of administration, has imposed limits upon concessions and restricted this German policy to a nominal degree of execution."

The "bulwark" had been purely a propaganda ploy, sterile, inadequate, and unimpressive. It was no temptation for the Vatican. During all this campaign, the Reich government never approached the Vatican, either by appeals in the press or through diplomatic channels. Hitler had long since gotten himself into the habit of systematically ignoring the Pope. As will be seen in a following chapter on the history of the diplomatic mission of Ambassador Weizsäcker in the Vatican, Hitler made no move to enlist Pius XII in his effort to "save Europe". Like Sapieha, why should the Pope intervene to save Nazism, even against the Bolsheviks, without signs of repentance?

Chapter 16

DIPLOMATIC RUSH FOR
"NEGOTIATED PEACE" IN 1943

Diplomacy takes its own course, by its own rules, regardless of propaganda, although never without reference to propaganda. While Dr. Goebbels was battling with windmills in the press and radio, the chancelleries were coming to grips with the new situation on the level of action. With the visible faltering of the German war machine at the start of 1943, the never-ending pursuit of peace took on new life. Neutral diplomats not unreasonably thought that the Stalingrad setback might stir in the Nazi leadership some thoughts of negotiation. Almost immediately the German reverses raised the image, among the Nazi satellite states in Eastern Europe, of a German withdrawal putting them in jeopardy. Italy and the lesser Axis allies, such as Finland, Slovakia, Rumania, Hungary, and Bulgaria, already had a mind to get out of the war. The moment had come to push farther in this direction. Those neutral countries considered favorable to the United Nations allies, such as Switzerland, Sweden, and Portugal, had a less direct involvement, but they had a certain stake, politically and otherwise, in promoting negotiations. Other neutral countries more linked to the Axis, such as the collaborationist Vichy France and the Spain of Generalissimo Francisco Franco, found the prospect of a German defeat quite disturbing. For Spain the threat of a sovietized Europe was too real to be treated lightly. It was not necessary for Dr. Goebbels to insist with Spain on the Red peril.

The diplomats were on the march in 1943. They urged

"negotiations". The Rumanian foreign minister, Mihail Antonescu, came to Rome while the Stalingrad battle was coming to its foreseeable climax. Count Ciano recorded on January 19 that the visitor told the Fascists that the Italians might need to make contact with the United Nations allies "to search for a defense against the Bolshevization of Europe". The Swiss, too, went into action. Could not the neutrals unite in some kind of demarche in a joint call for negotiations? On February 10, the chief of foreign affairs of the Political Department, Marcellin Pilet Golaz, called Nuncio Archbishop Filippo Bernardini to his office and asked him whether it was not time "for the neutrals and for the Holy See to reach an understanding, with the scope of impressing on both belligerents the gravity of the danger and the necessity of peace". Switzerland, reported the nuncio to the Vatican, had in mind action by Sweden, Spain, and Portugal as well as Switzerland and the Vatican. Bernardini wrote again a week later, February 18, that the Lithuanian, Hungarian, Spanish, Greek, Polish, and Brazilian representatives in Bern in private conversations with him unanimously shared the Swiss view of the situation. (But he did not say they had agreed to any joint action.) The German ambassador to the Holy See, Diego von Bergen (about to retire), got wind of the Swiss appeal to the Vatican and so reported to the Foreign Ministry in Berlin. Ribbentrop's answer was unhelpful and uncompromising: "Germany thinks of war, not peace!"

Contrary to what perhaps some might have expected, the Vatican did not hasten to take up the Swiss idea of a joint demarche. On March 3, the cardinal secretary of state, Luigi Maglione, wrote to the nuncio:

> Your Excellency knows how much the august Pontiff longs for the conclusion of a just peace. You can therefore be assured that the Holy See follows the situation with attention. I should add that, unfortunately, it sees nothing at the present moment that permits it to hope, for the immediate future. If nevertheless some possibility should appear on the horizon, the Holy See would be more than happy to work for the hoped-for peace.

Cardinal Maglione did not explain why the Holy Father did not think there were "at the present moment" grounds to hope for an early peace. At the time of his 1942 Christmas allocution, it was noted, perhaps with surprise, that he made no call for peace, for negotiations. Although peace feelers had come to him, for example, by way of Franz von Papen in Turkey, the Pope detected no yielding in Berlin, certainly none by way of the Reich ambassador to the Holy See. The Nazis were pushing the Communist danger, but not to the point where they were willing to discuss a negotiated peace on this basis. The Allies in the West themselves were equally intransigent. Myron Taylor in his talks with the Pope had categorically sworn, in the name of President Roosevelt, that there could be no negotiated peace with Hitler—certainly no separate peace in an anti-Soviet sense.

The Swiss attempt had no followup. But in Spain, Generalissimo Franco took a strong initiative on his own. This was in the form of an appeal, first, directly to the British and later to the world public, in favor of an early peace in view of the Communist threat, in the wake of Germany's growing weakness. On February 28, the British ambassador in Madrid was given a "secret memorandum" that expanded on the Bolshevization of Europe consequent on a German defeat. Germany, it was said in the document, is "the sole power existing in the center of Europe capable of realizing the great universal work of struggle". Do you want, wrote Franco, to count on a confederation of Lithuanians, Czechs, Poles, and Rumanians who would quickly become one more state of the Soviet Union? Communism, he went on, is the major danger of the world. "Who is going to save Europe from it—France? If the Russians conquer Germany, nothing will save Europe. A long war profits nobody. The greatest service we can perform for Europe consists in not losing the opportune moment for peace." The generalissimo delivered a speech on March 17 to the newly assembled Cortès on the danger of a war that exhausted both sides. The Spanish foreign minister, Francisco Jordana, added to this, in a speech in Barcelona on April 16. Spain, he said, wished to prepare this peace, in the measure possible. He did more than hint that he expected the Holy See to intervene. "The Holy See, which keeps watch with such love over the good of humanity and the nations spared by the war, could without any doubt facilitate the coming of this peace and collaborate in the preparation of treaties in contributing its equitable and disinterested point of view." Franco, in another address at Almeria on May 9, said that Spain wished to "raise its voice in union with that of the Sovereign Pontiff, to appeal to the conscience of the peoples".

Jordana's speech made a great impression in Vichy, arousing even feverish speculation. Diplomats and correspondents were sure that the Pope would echo these ideas in his forthcoming Easter allocution. But Easter (April 25) came and went without the Pope taking cognizance of what was in the minds, and on the lips, of so many.

What was the thinking of Pius XII at this springtime, post-Stalingrad, crisis in international relations? His reticence and his distancing from peace talks appeared contrary to what could be expected of him, notably concerning the Communist danger. Was he so indifferent? In reality the situation was not so simple for the Holy See as it seemed to European opinion. In these very weeks, on March 2, the Vatican had sent to the Reich government a long protest against Nazi persecution in Poland. It was of such gravity that Pius XII could well have expected a rupture of relations. It had been in preparation for over a year, long before the Nazi star began to fade at Stalingrad. The document was dry, factual, even austere, but devastating. It avoided phrases that, however justified, could have provided Hitler with a pretext for rejecting it as "Political Catholicism" or interference in matters that did not regard the Church. The Reich had no alternative but to squirm and ignore it. It remained a secret, its very existence unknown until after the war, when it was supplied by the Vatican itself for the use of the International Military Tribunal at Nuremberg. The Pope had no desire to see his protest in defense of the Church, and particularly in Poland, become a plaything for the propaganda of either side, even after Berlin's rejection.

Had it become known in 1943, it would have been a veritable propaganda bomb. Even the Poles, directly concerned and always keeping a close eye on the Vatican's stand, never learned of it.

The hard-driving March 2 letter was weighing on the Pope's mind as a decisive act of his pontificate when he received a very long letter dated February 24 from the Hungarian prime minister, Nicholas de Kallay. To buttress his case, the premier had some adviser in the country draw up, ostensibly for his own use, a list of all past papal condemnations of Communism. He also held up the grim specter of a conquered Germany united with Moscow in a separate peace to form "the greatest and most hateful world power, the Russian-German Communist Union". The diplomat concluded by begging the Pope to "continue the struggle against Communism on the example of his predecessors".

In his reply, or comment, on the cry of alarm from Hungary, Pius XII on March 7 told the Hungarian minister Gabriel Apor: (1) "The Holy See has not closed its eyes to the Communist danger" and (2) "It is not possible to renew publicly the condemnation of Bolshevism without speaking at the same time of the persecution under way at the hands of the Nazis." Kallay came to Rome soon after, and the Pontiff had the chance, in an audience accorded the premier on April 3, to develop his thoughts more in detail. Kallay recorded:

> In front of His Holiness lay the letter which I had addressed to him on March 1 [*sic*], concerning the dangers of Bolshevism. Using the letter as a lead, His Holiness brought up the matter of conditions in Germany. He depicted the conditions prevailing in Germany, which fill him with great sadness, in dramatic words. He finds incomprehensible all that which Germany does with regard to the Church, the Jews, and the people in the occupied territories, first of all the Poles. These measures not only are interference in the affairs of the Church but also are in opposition to the principles of a Christian world order based on the word of God.
>
> He is filled with sadness all the more because, it seems to him, these measures have to such an extent poisoned the atmo-

sphere between Germany and the Anglo-Saxon powers that these latter regard all attempts at detachment from the war as vain so long as Germany and the German occupation authorities disregard the most elementary principles of human and moral laws. Of this he had become convinced as a result of conversations with Myron Taylor and others.

He is quite aware of the terrible dangers of Bolshevism, but he feels that, in spite of the Soviet regime, the soul of the large masses of the Russian people has remained more Christian than the soul of the German people.

Under such circumstances the Church does not have the opportunity to intervene. Germany, having abandoned all humane lines of policy, has, instead, pursued a policy that arouses complete mistrust on the other side. That is, as long as inhuman tendencies prevail in Germany, he can see no possibility for the Church to mediate between the belligerents.

Kallay's official record of this remarkable papal statement, so revealing for the thinking of Pius XII, was duly consigned to the archives of the Hungarian Foreign Ministry, after which it ended in American hands. The Pope's words indicated clearly to his visitor that the Holy See was not prepared to launch an anti-Bolshevik drive in the sense of Kallay without any reference to the record of Nazi Germany. Further, the Pope found himself blocked from his hopes to be a mediator among the warring nations. Until Germany ceased its inhuman policies or gave some signs of a change, a papal intervention was out of the question. This was in April 1943.

Nicholas de Kallay's own memoirs, published after the war, outlined his exhortations to Pius XII in these terms:

> I pointed out that, while even the Church's visible struggle was being waged against atheism and while that struggle would end by the victory of the West for Christianity, the great threat against Christianity was from the East. The victory of the Allies would mean a Communist victory as well, and then woe to Protestants and Catholics alike, because Russia had never been either of these.

These words refer solely to Kallay's letter of February 24, not to his private audience of April 3, which possibly for diplomatic correctness he chose not to cite.

Was all this diplomatic fever—from which the Vatican stood aloof, despite open invitations—simply a "peace offensive" created by Hitler and Goebbels? The British organs, accustomed to ferreting out such tactics, tended to attribute the Swiss, Hungarian, Spanish, and French manifestations of these months to a not too subtle Berlin maneuver. The neutrals' interventions seem rather to have annoyed Berlin not a little as an unwelcome political initiative in its zone of influence. The Reich was ready to exploit the Bolshevik menace, but only to rally resistance, not as a prelude to negotiations. The Nazi leaders shrank from an open peace bid of their own, which could be seen as a sign of weakness. They had no choice but to wait hopefully for an Anglo-American or Soviet invitation, whichever made the better offer. All they could do was to foment mutual distrust among the Allies, which could lead to a split in the victorious coalition.

The Germans themselves insisted on "no compromise". After the Jordana speech of April 19 a Berlin spokesman said that nothing was known of any move by the Spanish government "to offer its services in peace negotiations". And he added, "Germany's standpoint on this question is clear. Germany will only consider a victory without compromise."

Attitudes remained fixed in this position. It was to end in May 1945 with the occupation of the capital of the "thousand-year Reich" by the Red Army. But two years had yet to run.

Chapter 17

"UNCONDITIONAL SURRENDER"

The wartime alliance or coalition among the Soviet Union and the Western powers was a marriage forced by circumstances on incompatible partners whose chief bond was a common external enemy and hence kept alive by military necessity. If Stalin accepted military and economic aid, it was almost as if he would have preferred to fight—and lose—the war all by himself rather than enter into too close relationships with the class enemy in the West. It required a hurried patching over of mutual long-standing hostilities to get that coalition going. Like most wartime coalitions, it barely survived the war, and when the Nazi specter vanished in the smoke of the Berlin Reichschancellery, the old pattern reasserted itself. Ancient Russian ambitions in the Middle East and in the Balkans came in collision with British interests. More significantly than power considerations, the end of the war saw Europe reeling on the verge of another "new order", that of world Communism. Who could say in 1945 that history would not repeat itself and Bolshevism's hour might have arrived also even for Western Europe? That was certainly the conviction of the Communist parties at work in the Resistance in France and in Italy. In Moscow the party theoreticians proclaimed again what they had never recanted: that there were still two camps—the bourgeois-capitalist and the Communist. Altogether it was a highly unsettling prospect. Out of it came the Cold War.

The instability of the "strange alliance" was on the minds of all the belligerents, especially by 1944, and even sooner. To exploit this potential split in enemy ranks, for example, by rumors of a "separate peace" with the one or the other, was a central task of the Nazi propagandists. For the same reason, hush-hushing of tensions within United Nations' ranks was imperative. The very real possibility that Hitler might succeed in splitting the United Nations (as the coalition was now called) possessed Winston Churchill. The British were mortally afraid of talk of a "negotiated peace", that is, an attempt by Hitler to demoralize the enemy through a pretended desire to settle with the West—at the expense of the Soviet Union. Or with the East—at the expense of the British and the Americans. After the traumatic turnovers of Berlin-Moscow relations in 1939 and 1941, anything was conceivable. Were Hitler and Stalin capable of yet another about-face to come up with a "cease-fire"? After years of broken pledges and bad faith, the Führer's credibility was nil with the British. A peace move from that quarter could only be put down as a dangerous maneuver. However, to the suspicious Stalin, a British-German secret agreement, in an anti-Soviet sense, was also within the realm of possibilities.

The curious incident of alleged negotiations on the Spanish-French border was enough to underline Stalin's fear of betrayal. The long delay in launching the "second front" in France appeared to him as a plot to let the Red Army bleed to death in solitary combat. Suddenly, on January 18, 1944, *Pravda* came out with a dispatch, allegedly from Cairo, according to which British agents had met envoys of Ribbentrop in the Pyrenees, where conditions for peace were discussed. Nothing further has ever been heard of this meeting, evidently wholly invented. Even at the time it was seen as a palpable Kremlin "fishing expedition". Indignant denials rose from London, amazement that Moscow could imagine such a thing, refusal to dignify it by a denial, and so on. It was easy for the British press to comment, under Foreign Office benevolence, that the story must have been a *Störmeldung*, put out by the Germans themselves, to poison Soviet-British relations. Presumably Stalin was momentarily assured of his ally's good intentions.

A mischievous interloper in the delicate drama was the Spanish dictator, Generalissimo Francisco Franco. He was bold enough to put in crude terms again what was unspeakable in those months. He urged Churchill to set the stage for a united Western front against the Soviets. He wrote this in a letter to the prime minister on October 18, 1944, transmitted by the Spanish ambassador in London:

> Since we cannot believe in the good faith of Communist Russia and since we know the insidious power of Bolshevism, we must take into account the fact that the weakening or destruction of her neighbors will greatly increase Russia's ambitions and powers, making necessary more than ever an intelligent and understanding attitude on the part of the Western countries.

That danger was exactly what the British did not want aired at that time, no matter how prophetic. Churchill interpreted the Franco letter as an appeal for a new *cordon sanitaire,* a new form of anti-Communist alliance. Mindful of the Anglo-Soviet Treaty of June 1942, he replied curtly as follows: "I should let your Excellency fall into serious error if I did not remove from your mind the idea that His Majesty's Government would be ready to consider any bloc of Powers based on hostility to our Russian allies, or on any assumed need of defense against them." This correspondence "from a Swiss source" was printed after the war by the *Times* of London on September 19, 1945. A leading article in the same issue described the Franco proposal as a "crude attempt to sow discord between allies by denunciations of 'Communist Russia' and the 'Reds' which bear the hallmark of Goebbels himself".

A few weeks later Churchill was out of office and free to say what he really thought, but not before ordering the British forces in Schleswig-Holstein to stockpile seized German weapons. This mysterious directive could have only one meaning—the intent to use ex-Wehrmacht troops in the event of a Red Army invasion of Western Europe. At Fulton, Missouri, in 1946 the ex–prime minister delivered his famous "Iron Curtain" speech. In 1947 President Harry S. Truman proclaimed the "Truman Doctrine" to contain Communism. In 1949 the North Atlantic Treaty Organization came into being, a defensive military alliance against the Soviet Union. What was howled down in 1944 became permanent democratic policy, lasting until the collapse of Communism many years later.

The Holy See was a very concerned outsider as this high policy issue ran its course. The Allied diplomats at the Vatican insisted that the war would be prosecuted with determination, to the complete extinction of the National Socialist regime, with which no negotiations were possible. This was a subtle but effective way of telling the Pontiff not to keep telling them of the bad consequences of Versailles. For its part, the Vatican could assure the diplomats that it was of course by no means in favor of "peace at any price", if that was what was implied by "negotiation" or "a compromise peace". Real peace was the fruit of justice. In 1942 it was noted by the press that Pius XII in his recent addresses had virtually suspended his once-conspicuous peace appeals. Vatican Radio said that "from Dunkirk to Salerno" the Pope had avoided the subject because he saw no real possibilities of negotiations at that time.

But from 1943 on, the papal tone changed. Possibly a proximate cause was the Roosevelt-Churchill enunciation at Casablanca in January 1943 of the policy of "unconditional surrender". This was an elaboration of "no negotiated peace". It raised doubts and created difficulties. What did it really mean? Churchill gave it only a reluctant consent, and, truth to tell, even Stalin disapproved of it, as he had his own plans for Germany. It was the personal idea of President Roosevelt, who borrowed the phrase from a situation in the American Civil War. Strange to say, the phrase did not appear in the final communique but got its prominence through a press conference of Roosevelt at the close, on January 24. It caught the imagination, stirring both praise and criticism. It was argued that the German people should not be led into thinking they were surrendering on some vague promises of the victors. That had occurred, it was recalled, at the close of the First World War. It was better not to make any promises, to keep one's hands free, rather than provide a pretext for later cries of false pledges. In contrast, the use that Goebbels made of the formula only hardened resistance, both in the military and on the home front. Subsequently, various efforts were made on the Allied side to modify the sense of the phrase, but the damage was done. Though at the time, and after the war, ardent supporters of the official policy defended the formula, there were not lacking influential and knowledgeable personalities who flatly avowed "unconditional surrender" to have been a bad slip. In 1949, for instance, the then foreign secretary in London, Ernest Bevin, told the Commons it had been a "very great mistake", adding that he himself, though in the government, had learned of it first from the newspapers.

More impressive is the testimony of General Dwight D. Eisenhower. It was not until years later, in an interview with a correspondent of the *Washington Post* of December 20, 1964, that the ex–supreme commander in Europe and ex–President of the U.S. stated that the Casablanca formula was indeed a mistake. It had, he said, prolonged the war and cost lives that otherwise might have been spared: "Hitler used something from the mouth of our own leader and persuaded the Germans to fight longer than they might have. I have always believed that the war should have ended sixty or ninety days before it did."

Governments naturally have their own tabus. Allied diplomats at the Vatican in the First World War had orders to keep the Pope (Benedict XV) from talking on peace. One can imagine why—the German army was still on French soil. And so, in 1942 it was the task of their successors at the Vatican to stifle anything that could in their judgment give aid and comfort to the Axis, above all in the area of peace talk. Pius XII in the main conducted himself, as far as the Allies (the British and Americans) were concerned, satisfactorily enough. They complained mainly that the Pope was not enthusiastic enough for the Allied cause, for example, by not excommunicating Mussolini or Hitler. Some in the Foreign Office put him down in the record as "a miserable weakling". Sometimes, in fact, they suspected that behind a papal statement stood Mussolini, if not Hitler. This was a fixation to which the British were particularly vulnerable. For them, the Pope was something like the archbishop of Canterbury in relation to the government. When that high prelate spoke, it was likely that the King (or, better, the Foreign Office) prompted him to say the right thing. In all fairness, it should also be understood that the Pope had to be careful that his words might equally be read in the Axis camp as inspired in turn by the British or the Americans. It was a particular annoyance to the Allies that the Pontiff did not view the cause of peace in quite the same way as they did. Consequently, at times the Pope said things that cut across the momentary strategy or current propaganda of the diplomats.

How long, for instance, could the Holy Father avoid the question that was in reality in the minds of everyone, the question of an early end of the war? Pius XII broke through the embargo in a speech he delivered on June 2, 1943, on the occasion of the feast of his patron saint, Eugenio. He lamented the prevalence of misunderstandings, of distortions of his words and of his intentions. Moral judgments, he regretted, were being made on the basis not of law and charity but of partisanship: "Those who have the power could offer nothing greater, nothing more noble, and necessary, nothing more glorious and more beneficent than the olive branch of peace."

In the same allocution the Pope also spoke of other aspects of the war: the bombings of cities without discrimination between military and civilian targets, the plight of the Jews ("those suffering by reason of their nationality or their race"), and likewise the sufferings and hopes of the Polish people. But this was submerged, as far as the press was concerned, by his unwelcome call for peace, surrounded though his words were by circumlocutions.

The incorrigible Pope returned to the call for peace soon again, in a radio address of September 1, the same year. It was on the occasion of the fourth anniversary of World War II. Could he speak without expressing his hopes for an early end of the interminable conflict? "Real strength", he cried out, "has no fear of being generous." A year later, on the recurring occasion of his name feast, June 2, 1944, the Pope resumed the theme of what he called "the formidable problem", that is, of a just and durable peace. His advice: in every war, if one of the belligerents succeeds in reaching a clear and unqualified victory only by the power of the sword or other measures of irresistible force, he is in the physical position of dictating a peace, imposed by force. "But certainly, no one whose conscience is formed by the norms of true justice can see in such a precarious condition the name of a sure and farseeing wisdom."

The irritated press—and some Sunday preachers—in the West saw in these words and indeed the whole tenor of the Pope's 1944 address the call for a "soft peace" for Germany, if not a negotiated peace. In the mood of the time, this did not go down well. That the Pope made allowances for the punishment of war criminals— "just expiation for violent acts committed against persons or things not required by the conduct of the war"—did not satisfy public opinion at that moment. It was inconceivable to the general public that in the course of time, Germany would be a member of NATO, in a military alliance against Bolshevism.

Chapter 18

WEIZSÄCKER: FAILURE OF A MISSION

The Reich ambassador at the Vatican, Ernst von Weizsäcker, (1943–1945) diligently played the anti-Communist card, not with the Pope so much as with his own superiors in Berlin. For him it was the formula for peace, a possible way out of the desperate situation into which Hitler's mad policies had brought Germany. It was the time after Stalingrad, when thinking Germans had to contemplate defeat without seeming defeatist. Weizsäcker bombarded his Foreign Ministry with highly colored reports of how Pius XII was paralyzed by the thought of a Bolshevik hegemony in Europe, welcoming any move that could avert this destiny. In practice, the diplomat had a double objective: he needed to convince Berlin, even Hitler and Himmler, first that the Vatican was close to Nazi thinking on this point and could serve as an opening to negotiations with the British and Americans, and second to convince the Pope that he should induce the Anglo-Americans to welcome a separate peace with Nazi Germany. He failed on both scores. Hitler and his intimates were not ready or able to make peace through the Holy See, even to save the Reich from Communism. And Pius XII declined to be the channel with the British and Americans for such a hopeless initiative as a separate peace. The Pontiff's supposedly overweening preoccupation with the Bolshevik danger, depicted so dramatically by Weizsäcker as the touchstone of Vatican policy, proved nonexistent, imaginary.

Indubitably, an ambassador's dispatches from his station are of prime importance for the historical record. Of all official witnesses of his time and place, he ought to be the most qualified. At his post he is the recognized channel of communication between his government and the authority to which he is accredited. By the same token the diplomat on service abroad can have his own strategy, which he inculcates in his superiors. It does not always work. How many ambassadors have been recalled when their evaluation of the situation has not coincided with their superiors' ideas? A classic case was the recall of the U.S. ambassador to London, Joseph P. Kennedy, by President Roosevelt in 1940. His reports during the London Blitz on the future of Great Britain were too pessimistic for the White House. Weizsäcker was not recalled. As an experienced civil servant he knew how to phrase his dispatches in the perspective of his own personal ideas without tipping his hand. Weizsäcker had his own agenda and used his professional knowledge of the workings of the Berlin bureaucracy in order to carry it out. His dispatches from Rome in these last months of the war have to be read with that agenda in mind. He was playing a double game.

Ernst von Weizsäcker (his son Richard was to become President of the Federal Republic) had been state secretary of the Reich Foreign Ministry, that is, a civil servant, second only to Ribbentrop. In circumstances never spelled out but that can be guessed at, in early 1943 he chose to leave this responsible post, asking on his own initiative to be sent to the Vatican. That spot was open. The long-time incumbent ambassador, Diego von Bergen, had been ailing and wanted to resign. The transfer of such a high diplomat to the Vatican at such a moment was interpreted by the world press as the beginning of a "peace offensive" by Hitler, through the Pope. As far as Weizsäcker was concerned, this was indeed his personal intent. But it was not Hitler's or Ribbentrop's intent. They gave no instructions to their new envoy to this effect. It was rather the envoy who intended precisely to induce his superiors in Berlin—perhaps by some miracle of conversion—to look in the Vatican's direction for the "way out" on the best terms possible.

Hitler approved the appointment without visible diffidence.

He was too busy anyway with his disastrous conduct of military affairs. Possibly he thought this was just Ribbentrop's way of getting rid of an inconvenient collaborator. Hitler was satisfied with the general program outlined to him in a personal encounter — clichés in diplomacy known all too well to Weizsäcker: "reciprocal noninterference; no discussions of fundamental questions; no deals". Weizsäcker later in his memoirs admitted that Ribbentrop did not know why he asked for the Vatican post. He went on to say that if the minister had learned what he was up to he would have recalled him within two weeks of his arrival. So began a story of misleading dispatches and an underground, unauthorized search for peace with the Western powers through the Vatican. Did Ribbentrop ever see through Weizsäcker?

The new envoy presented his credentials to Pope Pius XII on July 4, 1943. He saw the last weeks of the Fascist regime and the following short weeks of the Badoglio government; he was at his post during the nine months of the German occupation. In June 1944, with the Allied liberation of Rome, he withdrew to Vatican City with some of his staff until the end of the war. As is known, he was tried by the Americans at Nuremberg for war crimes and sentenced to some years in prison. This was in the course of the "Wilhelmstrasse Trials" conducted by the Americans against the Reich Foreign Ministry. Since the minister himself had already been hanged by this time, his state secretary had to stand in the dock in his place. The Vatican had no grievances against him and indeed wrote letters of recommendation on his behalf at the time of his trial.

Weizsäcker's official mission did not go any farther than to maintain the unenviable existing situation, which was that of stalemate. Reference has been made earlier to the strong protest of March 2, 1943, which the Holy See sent to Berlin—and which was not answered. Weizsäcker knew perfectly well these circumstances and the disastrous state of German-Vatican relations at that time. Why then did he choose to go to Rome, where, as far as Hitler was concerned, there was nothing for him to do?

In Rome, Weizsäcker had two immediate preoccupations: (1)

to keep at a minimum the frictions that arose regularly—and the less Berlin heard about these the better; (2) to induce the Vatican to take some steps in the direction of peace negotiations with the Allies, in the sense of a "Western solution". For this he had to tranquilize Berlin by presenting the Pope as so frightened at the prospect of a Soviet hegemony in Europe that he would be willing to forget and forgive all the Nazi misdeeds of the past and present if it would avert this possibility.

The device Ambassador Weizsäcker used most consistently in his nearly two years at the Vatican was to highlight the Communist peril. This approach fitted perfectly into the current German propaganda. He let no occasion pass without emphasizing with his superiors how worried the Vatican Curia was about the possibility of the collapse of the Wehrmacht on the Eastern front. No fewer than nine of his dispatches have survived in which the Communist peril is dragged in, with increasing passion. The invariable theme was that the Vatican looked on the German forces as a heaven-sent barrier against the inroads of Bolshevism and, thus, by implication, that the Vatican would welcome an early peace with the Anglo-Americans before it was too late. In this way the West (that is, Nazi Germany included) could put up a solid front against the Soviet Union and its ideology. A brief review of each of these consistent dispatches will suffice to make the point.

The Communist problem emerged from the start. Reporting to Berlin after his first papal audience of July 4, he wrote, "The conversation, which lasted about a half-hour, was carried on by the Pope without visible emotion, but with an undertone of spiritual intenseness that showed a common interest with the Reich only with the discussion of the anti-Bolshevik fighters."

Is he saying that the Pope complained of everything and that the only point he could have in common with the Reich was the Communist problem? If so, it would not be the last time, nor was it the first, that the old civil servant chose to sweep under the carpet the catalogue of grievances that Pius XII had for so many years against the National Socialist Reich. When he was state secretary and had to face a protest from the papal nuncio, Archbishop Cesare Orsenigo, he would arrange to meet the prelate privately in a cafe outside the ministry. In that way he did not consider he had to put the Vatican's indignation on the written record, while assuring the nuncio he would do all he could. One can imagine what significant lacunae have resulted in the Vatican files of the ministry. It is impossible that the Pope, at such a moment, would have failed to bring up the Reich's ignoring of the March 2 protest. The ambassador practically tells us this. But for Weizsäcker there was no point in detailing such things to Berlin. By his own way of thinking he had said enough about the bad state of Church-state relations in the careful phrases of his account. Weizsäcker was capitalizing rather on Pius XII's known hope of being a factor for ending the war.

In the context of this study of the Pope and Communism, it is worthy of note that in the advance text of the address (prepared for him, with his participation, in the Foreign Ministry) that Weizsäcker was to deliver, the question of Communism was repeated several times. This text was rejected by Maglione as "too long". Weizsäcker gave a revised address without mentioning the word *Communism.*

A month later, on August 3, he wrote that the Pope's "greatest worry" was Bolshevism. Three weeks later still, on August 30, he developed his thought in a review of his two months' experience: "The Curia fears the Bolshevization of Europe, and this worry determines its policy today." Farther on, he added:

> The Soviet Union is and remains the archenemy [*Erzfeind*]. So it happens that in the Vatican these days there is no need for words to put the German effort against Soviet Russia in the correct light. But the Vatican is concerned because the limitless task of the defense of Europe rests on German strength, and the hope is that this defensive will not fail, in order to bring the war to a good conclusion, in order to head off the Bolshevik danger.

A few days later, on September 3, the ambassador reported information that he said he had received from an unidentified

Italian publicist, citing what the Pope had allegedly said when asked his opinion about the Germans: "It is a great people which in its fight against Bolshevism sheds its blood not only for its friends but also for its present-day enemies. I would not like to believe that the Eastern front will collapse."

Three more weeks. On September 23, the ambassador cited a document of unexplained origin that he said had come into his hands: "Maglione says that the fate of Europe hangs on the victorious resistance of the Germans on the Russian front. The German army was the only possible bulwark against Communism. If this should fail, it would be the end of European culture."

A dispatch dated immediately after, September 24, refers to the alleged Vatican preoccupation in a different perspective. Weizsäcker denounced rumors of a possible link between Berlin and Moscow. The Vatican, he said, was afraid of a sell-out to Russia: "Just as persistent, however, is the dream of the Vatican that the Western powers will recognize in time where their true interests lie and, in union with the German struggle, help save European culture from Bolshevism."

On October 8 came another affirmation that anti-Bolshevism remained the enduring element (*Bestandteil*) of Vatican policy in international affairs. "Whatever serves to fight Communism is welcome to the Curia", wrote Weizsäcker, adding that the papal Curia now saw no other hope against the Reds but Germany. Finally, he wrote on December 13, "Bolshevism is, and remains, the nightmare [*Alpdruck*] of the Pope. He hopes desperately that the German wall in the East will hold firm militarily. . . . The dream of the Pope is therefore the union of the old civilized nations of the West [*Abendland*] for the expulsion of Bolshevism to the East, somewhat like in the times of Innocent XI."

The example of Pope Innocent XI, who led a crusade against the Turks in the seventeenth century, was much in the ambassador's mind. In June 1945, when the war was over, he picked up his theme again with this description of Pius XII's mind: "Nothing could have been more welcome to the Pope than a common offensive [*Zusammengehen*] of the West with Germany against Bolshevism threatening from the East, somewhat as once Europe joined forces under Innocent XI against the Turks." The Protestant Weizsäcker shared with many other non-Catholics an outdated fascination for the notion of "crusade". The Pope, Weizsäcker believed or pretended to believe, would like nothing better than this kind of union of the West with Nazi Germany against the Soviet Union, in the name of a "crusade", as in mid-1941 it was supposed that nothing could please the Vatican more than Hitler's war on the Soviet Union. Weizsäcker persisted even after the war as a prisoner of his misconceptions.

Ambassador von Weizsäcker knew exactly what to say to his people without risking the charge of defeatism. He had to exaggerate a bit. He knew that his dispatches were also sent to other agencies, such as the party Chancery (Bormann), and to the police (Himmler). In reality, these repetitious dispatches are a veritable caricature of the way of thinking of Pius XII. He is portrayed as clinging like a frightened child to the National Socialists as the savior of the West. Why was the ambassador reduced to citing only third-hand witnesses and indirect sources, when he had constant personal contact with the Pope and with the Pope's most intimate assistants? If these responsible persons had really spoken in such terms, would not the German diplomat have shot the news immediately to Berlin? The fact is that Weizsäcker for his own purposes carefully refrained from reporting most of his conversations in the Vatican, as found in the Vatican's own documentation. This would have spoiled his game, bringing down upon himself a reprimand from Berlin for an unauthorized initiative.

Weizsäcker did not, for instance, report a conversation with the cardinal secretary of state, Luigi Maglione, on August 27, 1943. The cardinal put down what he told the diplomat:

As regards the danger of Communism, the Holy See has always been concerned about this and is even more preoccupied now because it sees it as imminent, because the unspeak-

able sufferings brought on by the war create the conditions for
Communist theories. Exasperated souls naturally turn more
and more to extremism. I did not conceal from the ambassador
that I speak often of this danger to the Anglo-Saxon diplomats.

It was as if Maglione were defending himself against the accusation he and the Pope were not anti-Communist enough. Weizsäcker
did not tell Berlin about this audience, for his own reasons.

On the German side Berlin never had the slightest wish to use
the Pope of Rome as a vehicle of rapprochement with the Anglo-
Americans. No instructions or encouragement of the kind came
to Weizsäcker to continue on his line. Hitler was sinking deeper
into the intransigence—the "Samson complex", as Weizsäcker
later described it—that had served him so well in the past. What
could he do in any case? Any gesture of "change" or compromise
of any kind would be interpreted by his own people as weakness,
with catastrophic consequences, hence no change or desire of
change in the harsh antireligious policy was visible. In fact,
Berlin seemed determined not to give any occasion for the world
to speculate. The papal nuncio got no "signals" from the ministry.
Not one priest, even a German, was released in these days from
Dachau as token of a wish to mend fences. Relaxation of persecuting legislation in the Reich, or of Gestapo harassment, was not
even hinted at. What could the Church expect from Hitler but a
new wave of persecution? Was the "Red terror" of a Bolshevik
occupation, still hypothetical, any worse than the "Brown terror"
of National Socialism already in progress?

Weizsäcker was an official of the Reich. When he spoke of
Germany, he had to be understood as meaning Nazi Germany.
The diplomat too easily passed over the serious situation of the
Catholic Church under Nazi power, and it was vain for him to
promise a better future in the Reich when the signs of change
were nowhere to be seen.

At a late stage, in February 1945, Ribbentrop, the foreign
minister, broke his immobilism to the point of threatening that if
the West did not make peace with the Reich (against the Soviets,

of course), the Reich itself would go Communist. This message was in a circular dispatch to the principal Reich diplomats in neutral countries. The Vatican embassy was one of the recipients. By this time the Vatican ambassador was fully disenchanted, and he replied, courageously and frankly for once, that there was no chance of an agreement with the West without what he euphemistically called a "change in personnel" in Berlin. (This is a sample of the cryptic language of Reich diplomats at this time.) He got as his reply that "there could be no question of a 'change in personnel' because only National Socialism can save Europe and Germany."

Ernst von Weizsäcker was at the end of his diplomatic tether. He made one more try to salvage his campaign for a peace negotiated through the Pope—with the West, against the Soviet Union. He saw Pius XII in private audience on March 1, 1945. Was there any possibility, he asked, of conversations with the Americans? The Pope told him that, "after having sounded the terrain, he had come to the conclusion there is no possibility of conversations or discussions with the United States and Britain." The order of the day was "unconditional surrender". It was Weizsäcker's last move. He had failed in his grand personal strategy. Did he think that the Pope did not care if Germany was overrun by the Bolsheviks or if the whole country went Communist?

Chapter 19

"CATHOLIC COMMUNISTS": THE CASE OF FRANCO RODANO

The end of the war in 1945 found the Soviet Union and the Communist movement itself in a favorable position such as had never before been enjoyed in its existence. The Communists could only profit from the impressive military successes of the Red Army. A wave of goodwill swept through the ranks of the victors in the West. The meeting of the Big Three (Roosevelt, Churchill, and Stalin) at Yalta in February was indicative enough of the future shape of world politics. There was a place for the Soviet Union in the new international community. It had been a long war, and so much had changed. New ideas, new attitudes, had to be developed. Optimists in the West thought that this was the right moment for the free nations to reconsider their opposition to that "bogey" in Russia. In the euphoria of victory and the crashing downfall of Nazism, no one thought of a return to the *cordon sanitaire* policy by which the powers after the First World War sought to encircle and seal off the Bolsheviks. No one, that is, outside the Soviet Union. Stalin had his own ideas. If there was any "sealing off" to be done, he was the one to do it. Even less was there taste for, or consideration of, another war, a turning of the front, which the military in Germany had conceived as a possible solution to their predicament. The optimists in the West also watched with high interest the signs that Stalin might be in the mood to depart from the rigid Marxist-Leninist guidelines once controlling Soviet policy. Was Stalin about to renounce his dearly held ideology, the class conflict, the revolution? Was old Russia about to come to life, reawakened by the war sufferings? Every little sign to confirm this hope was zealously collected by the Western press, for example, changes in the Red Army. Political commissars were officially eliminated; old war heroes of the Czarist times were brought back into honor; an officer corps was reestablished. These were hopeful signs of a return of the Russia that Europe once knew.

No one really knew, but so many hoped it was true. In the meantime, what was happening in Britain and France? Socialism became the vogue. Britain, hardly had the war ended, brought the controlled economy to the fore, beginning with the nationalization of the major industries. The announced policy of "austerity", meaning, in reality, more rationing, was accepted by the population, already habituated to wartime shortages. The program of nationalizations was imitated in France, with doctrinaire bureaucratic dedication to the controlled economy.

But the European economy after six destructive years remained in a bad condition, stagnant. Recovery was exasperatingly slow, despite or because of the nationalizations. (Occupied Germany could not and did not contribute to the economic revival, for the known political reasons.) Social unrest, class warfare, loomed. Revolution was in the air. The "working class" was on the march. The ranks of the Communist party in France swelled. Could not Marxism-Leninism do better? This was certainly the conviction of party ideologues, who were sure the end could not be anything else than the rising of the proletariat—which they did their best to hasten.

After two years it was evident that Europe was on the verge of dangerous political instability. In June 1947 the U.S. secretary of state, General George C. Marshall, announced unexpectedly and almost casually that the United States was ready to come to the aid of the European countries financially, if they could agree among themselves on a common general plan of recovery. It was the Marshall Plan.

The Plan, it is good to recall, was not announced in an

anti-Soviet sense, and the new regimes in Eastern Europe, called "popular republics", were equally invited. But as far as Stalin was concerned the American move was an intrusion into his own sphere of influence, with all kinds of dangerous implications. He had no interest in salvaging the tottering capitalist economy of Europe and even less in allowing capitalism to infiltrate his own backyard. He abruptly ordered the overeager countries under his control, for instance, Czechoslovakia, to retract their acceptances. Moscow had its own plan—for the sovietization of Eastern Europe. The honeymoon was coming to an end. Then came the Stalinist coup of Prague in the spring of 1948, which opened eyes. In a matter of months, a year after the Marshall Plan, the United States inspired the creation of the North Atlantic Treaty Organization (NATO), a military alliance against a Soviet military threat. America had at last filled the power vacuum that, in the final analysis, was the root cause of Europe's economic and ideological predicament.

In the intellectual world the tendency was strongly in favor of Marxism. The strong drive for nationalizations reflected the conviction that the capitalistic system was at an end. Within the Catholic world, too, the temptation was strong to identify with the current trends. The movement among Catholics was particularly manifest in France. But it was in Italy, struggling to liberate itself from the relics of Fascism, that the "Catholic Communists" made their open entry onto the religious and social scene, under the banner of Communism.

One of the first manifestations of the new thinking developing in young Catholic intellectual circles was the letter that on December 13, 1942, Professor Carlo Piersanti, who was president of the Roman lyceum in the heart of Rome called the "Visconti", sent piously to the Pope, in the name of the faculty and students. He asked for recognition of a Christian, nonatheist, Communism:

> If your predecessor of happy memory piously and wisely condemned *atheistic* Communism [his italics], we pray that there may come, not an atheistic, but a Christian Communism,

to bring relief to humanity now so afflicted. In the new order
that we await let us be what the soul of the Christian is for the
body. Let us now prepare ourselves in mind and heart for such
a task.

This was an early formulation of a vague utopia that in the
months and years ahead was destined to be enlarged and refined
by the young students of the Visconti. It was not a movement in
competition with the clandestine Communist party but on the
contrary an effort to provide the basis for agreement. It implied
nothing less than the reform of Communism as it had been
known in Italy—and everywhere else. It was more than a pious
project. As was to be seen, the sponsors seriously misread the
signs of the times. It exemplified the state of war and postwar
ideological confusion that reigned everywhere, not only in Italy.
It was the extreme wing of the "Christian left", a continuing
political current to which Italian Catholic philosophers, such as
Francesco Malgeri, have dedicated conscientious research.

The case of Franco Rodano synthesizes the rise and the destiny
of the Catholic Communists. He was one of the group centered
in the Visconti, and he was also the very last. He had all the
credentials of an ardent Catholic Actionist, but he persisted in
following his chosen path of which he was so convinced. To the
end of his life he remained a dedicated "Catholic Communist"
and party member, despite his Church's condemnation. As a
significant incident in the ideological war in Rome itself, it
deserves recounting. It was a new test for the reigning Pontiff,
Pius XII, as the war reached its climax in Italy.

Rodano was only twenty-four when in May 1943 he was
arrested by the Fascist police for revolutionary activity. He had
come in contact already in 1940 with the clandestine Communist
party. Released from jail with the fall of Mussolini in July, he
proceeded to found the "Movement of Catholic Communists",
or the "Party of the Christian Left", with other Catholic youths
of like convictions. Rodano gave up this formula in December

1945. He became an influential theoretician at the side of the party secretary, Palmiro Togliatti.

The young Rodano was convinced that Communism was destined to be the force for the future, and he was able, to his own satisfaction, to close his eyes to the antireligious and anti-Christian tenets of Marxism-Leninism. He continued to dream of reconciling Catholicism with Communism. In 1973 his strategy of the "historical compromise", envisaging a Communist entry into the government with Catholic help, shook Italian politics. But its moment passed. In the end, if Franco Rodano had any influence it was in the realm of ideas among other youths coming after him and, like himself, born to navigate against the mainstream.

Rodano and his associates of the Movement of Catholic Communists set themselves resolutely to isolate Marxism-Leninism from its atheistic and materialist foundations. They were sure they had found a formula to make this possible. They were not the first, or the last, to try to build a bridge between the Christian concept of life and the Communist vision. They accepted, however, the main points of the Communist reform, making abstraction, somehow, from the ideological presuppositions. They certainly had no time for the Catholic social reform as it had been elaborated in the decades since Leo XIII. They set forth their goals, which, in their mind, offered the answer to the call of the hour. It never got any encouragement from the Pope, even though some priests were drawn into the cause. And it remained a minuscule movement. Some of its disillusioned partisans became prominent members of the Christian Democratic party.

The liberation of Rome in mid-1944 permitted the Christian Communists to come out into the open with their radical program. They issued their own newspaper. The Vatican's reaction did not delay in coming. The semiofficial newspaper *L'Osservatore Romano* of July 23, 1944, carried a front-page article by the Dominican theologian Mariano Cordovani, an authoritative exponent of Vatican thinking, under the interrogative "Catholic Communists?" The article bore heavily on the fact that the new movement discarded the whole Catholic social program in favor of the main points of the Marxist reform. The writer's point of departure was the booklet they had just issued, "Communism and the Catholics". It was a 143-page production in small print, which the anonymous authors were proud to announce had been printed clandestinely, *"alla macchia"*, in May 1944, that is, under the German occupation. The Catholic philosopher Augusto Del Noce was to call this the "Manifesto of 1944". Wrote the Dominican theologian:

> Some young Italians, attached to the most hardy ideas, have united for a movement of social reform with the name of "Catholic Communists". They wish to remain Catholics, and they reject the dialectical materialism of Communism as absolutely un-Christian. But they accept historical materialism regarding politics as an exercise of force. They call for the abolition of the private ownership of the means of production, with the aim of intensifying the private means of consumption; they intend to abolish social classes, except that of the industrial proletariat, which will take power into their hands, exercising violence and dictatorship to the point where a "socialist" society will be created, without class, in which there will be no capitalism, no luxury, and no misery. There will be no war, and all will be well.

One of the firsthand observers of Franco Rodano and the "Catholic Communists" at work as early as 1943 was the future many-times prime minister, Giulio Andreotti. He was then the youthful president of FUCI, the Federation of University Catholic Students, a part of Catholic Action. As such he was as much preoccupied with the future political course of Catholics as Rodano himself. A report that he prepared at the time on the early phases of the Rodano movement has come down, and it witnesses in concrete detail the drama that was developing in the rising generation of politically conscious post-Fascist Catholic youth. In the end of May 1943 the Fascist police in Rome arrested twenty students (including Rodano) on the charge of conspiracy. In fact, they were a group belonging for the most part to the youth branch of Italian Catholic Action. "The arrested", wrote Andreotti in a paper that ended up in the contemporary reports of American intelligence in Rome, "were members of a movement fundamentally Communistic, with Catholic tendencies and inspiration, at the head of which was one of the arrested, Franco Rodano, a university student for the doctorate of letters and a member of the Jesuit Sodality of Our Lady called 'della Scaletta' ". Andreotti went on to say that Rodano and the others were morally irreproachable in every phase of their personal lives, although at the university they fostered "social ideas that were more than daring and opposed to the teaching of the Popes".

Andreotti bestirred himself for their release, even getting the Vatican secretary of state to intervene for them. They had the "absolute conviction" that Communism would prove dominant in a great part of the world, including Italy, and they wanted, as believing Christians, to prepare themselves and the Catholic Church for the eventuality of a Communist ascendancy. They were ready and willing to reject atheism and dialectical materialism, but they were equally disposed to accept the Communist program of radical social reform. We can put this in Andreotti's own words:

> They blindly believed in the coming of Communism as a harbinger of a historical process, and they wished to garb that Communism with an aspect of Christianity. In order to do so, they mounted a criticism of the basis of the philosophy of Christian social doctrine as it is usually presented, not sparing criticisms of members of the ecclesiastical hierarchy, whom they often described as mediocre and inadequate.

On June 13, 1943, at the time when Rodano and the others were still in police hands, the Pope was scheduled to give a talk to a large crowd of Catholic workers. Andreotti was aware that the Pontiff was concerned about the circulation of Communist ideas in these circles, and he was afraid that the position of the arrestees would be jeopardized if the Pope touched too closely on this subject. He wrote to the Pope of this risk, and to his relief the Pope did not make the allusions that he feared. A few days later a group of Catholic Action leaders were received by the Pope. As the last to kiss the Pope's hand, Andreotti heard Pius XII say to him, "We were very discreet, were we not?"

With July 25 and the fall of Fascism, the young Catholics were released, all the more convinced of the correctness of their Marxist analysis. It was thought in Christian Democratic circles that the group could be taken into their ranks, even if on the extremist wing. A vain hope. Wrote Andreotti, "Instead, a few days after the German occupation of Rome in September, there appeared the first number of an underground paper, '*Voce Operaia* — organ of the Catholic Communists'". It stated that the group adhered in full, without any reservation, to the political precepts of the Italian Communist party. Andreotti remonstrated with his friend Rodano but got no answer. Soon the "Manifesto of 1944" appeared. In the spring of 1944, with his traditional address to the Lenten preachers, Pius XII issued a paternal invitation to those Communist youths "who profess to be Catholics" not to forget the clear teachings of Pius XI on the relations between Christianity and Communism. In an audience with the Pope soon after, Andreotti had to tell the Pope that the appeal had had no effect. After the Liberation in June 1944, the *Voce Operaia* took violent stands against the party of the majority of Catholics, that is, against the Christian Democratic party. In September 1944 the Movement changed its name to "Christian Left party". In the end even this designation disappeared, and the members, with Rodano at their head, with some exceptions, simply joined the Communist party. The march of history, on which they staked so much, passed them by.

EPILOGUE

World War II put enormous strain on the Vatican. With roots in the populations of every belligerent or neutral, it was in a highly delicate situation. Certainly Pius XII had a very limited sphere of action. The moral and spiritual issues arising out of war were extraordinarily complicated, and, worse, few of the belligerents were psychologically able to recognize this. One of the greatest hazards for the Holy See was to lose its independence of action even in the sphere that was peculiarly its own.

The first challenge was not long in coming. It was a peremptory demand of the French government for the Pope to condemn the German invasion of Poland. The Poles expected no less. What could be more natural than the Pope to rise in condemnation? Within a few more weeks the Soviets, too, invaded Poland. The independent Republic of Poland had been eliminated by a flagrant double aggression.

Pius XII fended off this campaign. He risked being accused of being pro-German. At this stage nobody accused him of being "obsessed" with the Communist danger. It was only later that Communist writers explained that Hitler had intended to invade Poland in order to have it as a launching pad against the Soviet Union and had so told the Vatican. This was only one of the many absurd inventions that came out of Moscow.

The average person whose knowledge of things Catholic is generic can find it difficult to comprehend the actions and attitudes of the universal Church in great political crises such as a world war. It is too easy to read politics in everything. The religious motivation gets completely obscured. Even Catholics (especially politicians) who might be expected to have some perspective very often tend to view Church positions solely in the light of their own immediate, purely national concerns. In wartime that should not be surprising. Opinion is mobilized. In the supreme effort it takes an extraordinary degree of objectivity for even a Catholic to put himself in the shoes of the Pope. As a result, the wellsprings of Vatican policy in the face of such a profound turbulence in society remain obscured not only during the war but also afterward. That was the experience Pius XII had to endure, but he was not the first. When his actions could not be criticized, his motives could be, with subjective criteria. Few are willing to give the Pope credit for being guided by purely religious motives. If his actions serve the national cause, they applaud. If they run against national interests, they criticize and denounce.

Even the sacrosanct cause of peace becomes the plaything of the belligerents. In both world wars the Holy See was warned by one or the other side not to speak of peace. It could sound defeatist or was demoralizing. A "peace offensive" was feared as a political trick. How many secret agents circulated in those days under the cover of searchers for peace? Some spies were there, but who could know? Yet presumably the prime preoccupation of wartime leaders is precisely to prepare for peace—their own, naturally, under the sign of "victory". What is left for the Pope, in time of war, as a spokesman for humanity, when his appeals for peace (or at least moderation) are so readily interpreted as partial and political, not to say sabotage, and hence to be ignored and denounced?

That there are often religious stakes in a war is indubitable. Sometimes it is said that the Catholic Church "lost" the First World War because it led to the dissolution of the Austro-Hungarian Empire of the Catholic Hapsburgs. Or, vice versa, that she "won" the war because it ended with the abdication of the Hohenzollern Kaiser, the bulwark of German Protestantism (not to speak of the Romanovs). Such is a crude, superficial, and materialist way of reading the religious, spiritual, and humanitarian aspirations of the Holy See in the great crisis.

It is more correct to see the Holy See's attitude as conditioned by the presence of forces of evil in the vesture of belligerent states. In World War II there were two such forces, the Soviet Union and the National Socialist Reich. Religiously the Pope's stance in their regard was clear. In October 1941 at the peak of Nazi power the intimates of the Pope heard Pius XII say, "A victory of the Axis would be the end of Christianity in Europe." A few months earlier he told a French cardinal in even more drastic terms, "If Germany wins the war, I believe it will be the greatest catastrophe to strike the Church in many centuries." If the head of the Catholic Church thought in this manner, why did he not say so in public and openly throw his moral support on the side of the United Nations? Was it even necessary, for those who had read the Pope's messages with any understanding? Welcome as such an explicit proclamation could have been to Roosevelt and Churchill, they and the public behind them would not have understood his words in the sense in which the Pope intended them. The statement would get a political interpretation — that is to say, it would be abused — in which the religious aspects would be completely lost in a flurry of propaganda and no good would be done, from the Papacy's point of view.

The supranational stance of the Holy See imposed upon the Pope certain courses of action, or of nonaction, which one or other of the belligerent parties was bound to misunderstand or, as the case may be, also to exploit. Every party concerned is likely to regard the Vatican as either implicitly friendly or implicitly hostile, according to whether it is felt that its actions help or hinder one's own cause. At a time when all energies converge on life-or-death politico-military aims of the war (including spiritual and religious energies), the mission of the Holy See comes very close to being either expropriated or wholly rejected.

The word *neutrality* is used too easily in this context and is inadequate when applied to the Papacy. It was never the proposition of the Holy See to close its eyes, or its mouth, on the religious, moral, and spiritual issues of the war, if in a language proper to its usages and its nature. The word *neutrality* does not express the situation of the Holy See in the face of the warring powers. The Vatican is not a Switzerland, a Sweden, or a Portugal, territorial entities with their own temporal interests. Even *impartiality* does not match the situation. Pius XII, more than ever in wartime, was deeply conscious, as Pope, that the Church was founded with a mission given her by Jesus Christ and subject to no earthly power. From this point of view the Church is an "idea", an abstraction, intangible, transcending politics. This of course is not understood, much less accepted, by the world's political forces. The Church is in the world but not of it. The implications of this came out forcibly during World War II. The Catholic Church is indebted to Pius XII for having consistently adhered to this fundamental conception, despite the enormous pressure that governments could and did exert on the Papacy. When World War II has receded into distant memory, the precedent of Pius XII will serve his successors in the See of Peter. Triumphalism? The highway of history is strewn with the wreckage of once all-powerful enemies of the Church.

BIBLIOGRAPHY

Alagiagian, Pietro. *Le mie prigioni nel paradiso Sovietico.* Rome: Paoline, 1956.

Benes, Edvard. *Memoirs: From Munich to New War and New Victory.* Boston: Houghton Mifflin, 1954.

Braun, Leopold. "Catholics behind the Iron Curtain." In *Worldmission* (Dec. 1950).

——. *Religion in Russia.* Newark, NJ: St. Anthony's Guild Press, 1959.

Christophe, Paul. *1939–1940: Les Catholiques devant la guerre.* Paris: Les Éditions Ouvrières, 1984.

Ciszek, Walter. *With God in Russia.* New York: America Press, 1964.

——. *He Leadeth Me.* San Francisco: Ignatius Press, 1995.

Cockburn, Patricia. *The Years of the Week.* Harmondsworth, 1971.

Déborine, Grigori. *La Deuxième Guerre Mondiale. Étude politique et militaire.* Moscow: Éditions en langues étrangères, s.d. (1955?).

Del Noce, Augusto. *Il Cattolico Comunista.* Milan: Rusconi, 1981.

Deschner, Karlheinz. *Abermals krähte der Hahn.* Stuttgart, 1962.

Doussinague, Jose-Maria. *España tenia razon (1939–1945).* Madrid, 1949.

Duclos, Paul. *Le Vatican et la Seconde Guerre Mondiale.* Paris, 1955.

Furet, François. *Le Passé d'une illusion.* Paris: Laffont-Caimana, Lóuy, 1995.

Hoettl, Wilhelm. *The Secret Front.* London: Weidenfeld and Nicholson, 1953.

Jaray, Gabriel Louis. *Pie XII, Messages de guerre au monde.* Paris, 1945.

Kallay, Nicholas de. *Hungarian Premier. A Personal Account of a Nation's Struggle in the Second World War.* New York, 1953.

Langer, William L. S. *The Undeclared War, 1940–1941.* New York: Harper, 1953.

Leoni, Pietro. *"Spia del Vaticano"!* Rome, 1959.

Lewy, Guenter. *The Catholic Church and Nazi Germany.* New York: McGraw-Hill, 1964.

Malgeri, Francesco. *La Sinistra Cristiana (1937–1954).* Brescia, Italy: Morcelliana, 1982.

Manhattan, Avro. *The Catholic Church against the Twentieth Century.* London, 1947.

McDonald, Iverach. *A Man of the Times.* London, 1976.

Mohr, Hubert, et al. *Katholische Orden und Deutsche Imperialismus.* Berlin, 1965.

Molnau, Kurt. *Aus dem Schuldbuch des politischen Katholismus.* Berlin, 1958.

Nicolle, Pierre. *Cinquant mois d'Armistice.* 1947.

Packard, Reynolds, and Eleanor Packard. *Balcony Empire, Fascist Italy at War.* New York, Toronto: Oxford University Press, 1942.

Piotrovski, Stanisław. *Hans Frank's Diary.* Warsaw, 1961.

Rosenberg, Alfred. *Der Mythus der XX Jahrhundert: Eine Wertung der Seelischgeisten gestalten Kampfe unserer Zeit.* Munich, 1933.

Rossi, A. *Une page d'histoire, Les Communistes français pendant le drôle de guerre.* Paris, 1951.

——. *La Guerre des papillons. Quattre ans de politique communiste (1940–1944).* Paris, 1951.

Schellenberg, Walter. *The Schellenberg Memoirs.* London, 1956. American edition: *The Labyrinth: Memoirs.* New York: Harper, 1956.

Schwabe, Matthias. *Der Kreuzzug der französischen Kardinäle.* Berlin, 1940.

Semmler, Rudolf. *Goebbels—The Man Next to Hitler.* London, 1947.

Sheinmann, M. M. *Der Vatikan im Zweiten Weltkrieg.* Berlin, 1948.

Sherwood, Robert. *Roosevelt and Hopkins: An Intimate History.* New York: Harper, 1948.

Taylor, Myron C. (ed.). *Wartime Correspondence between President Roosevelt and Pope Pius XII.* New York: Macmillan, 1947.

Weizsäcker, Ernst von. *Memoirs of Ernst von Weizsäcker.* Chicago, 1953.

Wenger, Antoine. *Rome et Moscou, 1900–1950.* Paris: Desclée de Brouwer, 1987.

Winter, Eduard. "Der Vatikan und Deutsche Imperialismus". In *Deutsche Imperialismus.* Berlin, 1953.

INDEX